Twists of Fate

Twists of Fate

Multiracial Coalitions and Minority Representation in the US House of Representatives

VANESSA C. TYSON

Oxford University Press is a department of the University of Oxford. It furthers
the University's objective of excellence in research, scholarship, and education
by publishing worldwide. Oxford is a registered trade mark of Oxford University
Press in the UK and certain other countries.

Published in the United States of America by Oxford University Press
198 Madison Avenue, New York, NY 10016, United States of America.

Library of Congress Cataloging-in-Publication Data
Names: Tyson, Vanessa C., author.
Title: Twists of fate : multiracial coalitions and minority representation in the
US House of Representatives / Vanessa C. Tyson.
Description: Oxford ; New York : Oxford University Press, [2016] |
Includes bibliographical references and index.
Identifiers: LCCN 2016004070 (print) | LCCN 2016016793 (ebook) |
ISBN 9780190250928 (hardcover : acid-free paper) | ISBN 9780190250935 (Updf)
Subjects: LCSH: United States. Congress. House—Membership. |
United States. Congress. House—Caucuses. | Minority legislators—United States. |
Coalitions. | Minorities—Political activity—United States. | Representative government
and representation—United States.
Classification: LCC JK1319 .T87 2016 (print) | LCC JK1319 (ebook) | DDC 328.73/0734089—dc23
LC record available at https://lccn.loc.gov/2016004070

9 8 7 6 5 4 3 2 1
Printed by Sheridan Books, Inc., United States of America

For my beloved Momo,
And the village that raised me

CONTENTS

ACKNOWLEDGMENTS

The completion of this project reflects the unwavering encouragement of many wonderful people in my life, in spite of various adverse circumstances. While I have countless individuals to thank, I will undoubtedly forget some here, and so I apologize in advance to those I inadvertently leave out.

First and foremost, I must give special thanks to my "dream team" dissertation committee, whose members provided endless guidance, support, and insight. Michael Dawson took a chance on this odd young woman from Southern California who constantly talked about minority politics and C-SPAN. I met Michael well before I applied to the University of Chicago Department of Political Science, and for over two hours straight we talked about black leadership and political history. His formidable knowledge about race, politics, theory, and history will forever inspire me to keep learning and growing as a scholar. Over the years, in Chicago and Cambridge and back again, the sage advice of Michael, and the late Alice Aiko Furumoto Dawson, would keep me grounded through my happiest moments and afloat during the most turbulent times as junior faculty. I'm forever grateful, and I wish Aiko were still here to read these words. Sometimes thank you comes too late.

I am also deeply indebted to the phenomenal Cathy Cohen, who served as a co-chair of my committee. Not only has her work impacted my understanding of the world and informed most all of the classes I teach, but her wisdom, tenacity, and humor make her an incomparable role model. Even though I consider her a friend, I am forever in awe of Cathy. I suspect my problematic procrastination at times came from a fear of submitting work to Cathy that was undeserving of her brilliance. My most sincere and heartfelt thanks is also owed to J. Mark Hansen and Eric Schickler, whose tremendous time and energy spent helping me refine this project will never be forgotten. I delight in knowing them both, and feel a tremendous gratitude for their sharing of an enviable wealth of institutional history combined with teeming insight into contemporary processes. The flaws in this project are mine, but its strengths are largely due to the knowledge these mentors bequeathed.

My academic family extends well beyond my committee, and as such I must acknowledge a number of people who encouraged me to continue on this path despite various hurdles and setbacks. Ange-Marie Hancock, you are the best big sister I never had! Your vibrant spirit is only paralleled by the brilliance of your mind and the kindness of your heart. You are a fantastic role model and a ride-or-die friend. I've also been blessed with a crew of slightly older, *infinitely* wiser scholars whose inclusion of me in their ranks kept me motivated: Mark Sawyer, Dara Strolovitch, Lester Spence, Melissa Michelson, Michael Leo Owens, Karthick Ramakrishnan, Cristina Beltran, Patchen Markell, and Ricardo Ramirez. This book reflects my effort to keep up. Additional thanks are most certainly due to Desmond King and Phil Klinkner, who offered much-needed advice and insight at various stages of the publication process.

My endless gratitude goes to my über-awesome editor at Oxford University Press, Angela Chnapko, a godsend unlike any other. My world (like the worlds of many promising scholars) has been a better place since the day we crossed paths, and I eagerly look forward to a lasting relationship. I also benefited from research assistance at various stages of the game, and I must thank Claudia Sandoval for her painstaking work on this project while she was an undergraduate at UCLA almost a decade ago, and Keytiana Hempstead for her brilliant indexing abilities during the spring of 2015 at UCLA.

Encouragement of my academic pursuits also came from the communities at two major research institutions. At Princeton University (where I completed my undergraduate work from 1994 to 1998), I have to thank the many professors of African American Studies, most notably Howard Taylor, Professor Emeritus of the Department of Sociology, who showed me tremendous kindness and helped me believe in myself and my research when I might have given up. Along with his brilliant, hilarious wife, Pat, Howie Taylor showed me the impact academics can make both in the lives of their students and in the world around them. Deans Nancy Kanach and Janina Montero saved me during some of my most turbulent times, and I'm thrilled my relationships with these two spectacular women have lasted over the years. Additional thanks must be given to Yina Moore, my beloved friend, cheerleader, and guru of all things, as well as the Association of Black Princeton Alumni—an organization that has enriched my life since 1997. Finally, I wish to acknowledge the tireless work of the staff in the Alumni Affairs Office.

At UCLA, where I served as a Visiting Assistant Professor in both African American Studies and Political Science as well as a scholar in residence, I am deeply indebted to the Institute of American Cultures, led by the indomitable Belinda Tucker, with the able assistance of Zella Johnson. Within the Institute, I must recognize the Ralph Bunche Center for African American Studies, directed by Darnell Hunt, whose steadfast commitment to the equal representation of persons of color in various media should inform us all. The faculty and staff at the Bunche Center welcomed me with open arms, and the warmth and kindness of Jan Freeman, Eboni Shaw, Ana-Christina Ramón, Dawn Jefferson, and Yolanda Jones had me grinning each day that I walked into work. Certain friends on campus also brought me tremendous cheer: Mark Sawyer (again), Janina Montero (again), Melvin Rogers, Ray Rocco, Lorrie Frasure, Tyrone Howard, and Jeff Lewis.

I feel enormous gratitude to the staff and alumni involved with the Junior State Foundation (JSA). Jeff Harris has been my fearless leader since I was fifteen years old. Wonderful people like Karen Prosser, Melody

Robidoux and Mick Thompson, Kip Morales, Gabriel Stempinski, Marty Barash, Jose Ugarte Peña, Matt Patchell, and Meghan Ginley provide me with laughter and insight into all things politics, society, and life. Meanwhile, the brilliant, determined high school students of JSA endlessly inspire me with their stories of courage, hope, and tenacity. Every day it is an honor and a privilege to be a part of such a worthy, diverse organization dedicated to civic engagement and public service. Becoming a member of JSA was unquestionably my best decision in high school, and staying involved as an adult remains an unparalleled blessing.

Words cannot describe my incredible fortune in knowing and adoring the Kaganoff Stern Tribe of Awesome, who fall into so many categories of support here that they constitute their own. First, to my beloved Sisters Kaganoff—Rachel and Tessa—I cannot imagine not having you both in my life and I'm so thankful for all of the kindness, warmth, and laughter you bring to my little world. You were raised by the fabulous Ann Kaganoff, aka "Grannie Annie," aka "Homegirl," so it is not surprising that you both are such phenomenal women. You made my return to Southern California a beautiful song of triumph and achievement. My unending adoration also goes to the amazing Stern men—Eric, Henri, and Jonah—who are equally fantastic in their own right, and light me up inside. You are all so very precious and I grin at the mere thought of you.

My blessings come in many forms, including a new position on the faculty of Scripps College, where I have the tremendous fortune of working with inspiring, supportive colleagues like Nancy Neiman Auerbach and the entire Department of Politics—I could not ask for better colleagues or a healthier, happier work environment. The leadership of Scripps includes the unstoppable Amy Marcus-Newhall, who leads with wisdom, finesse, and a firm backbone. Julie Liss has ably led the faculty as Interim Dean during my first year, and I'm extremely appreciative of her insight and generosity. The amazing staff of Scripps College, including Becky Rodriguez and Eleana Zeits, brighten my days immensely. In sum, the faculty, staff, and administration at Scripps show demonstrable strength at every turn, and I'm overjoyed to be a part of the intellectually rigorous Claremont Colleges.

Additional friends and loved ones provided me with much-needed support, encouragement, and the occasional room to rest my head: Tom Hayden and Barbara Williams, Bobby Scott, Rob Falk, Pamela Newkirk, Nancy and George Marquez, Mary Burschinger Levesque, Lizelda Lopez, Joo Young Lee, Laura Saslow, Kathy Anderson, the late Michelle Cormier and Dugan Bliss, Christie Garton and Matt Thompson, Colleen Shanahan and Mike Fischer, Wendy Landree, Frankie Waddy, Margo and David Simkin, and Shigenari and Kazuko Kimura. Although newer, the friendships of Brian Gott, Giselle Fernandez, Doug Holladay, and the PathNorth crowd provide me laughter and camaraderie, and reinforce my sense of purpose and commitment to community. Meanwhile, friends like Laurie Baulig, John and Jane Ransom, Vickie Kuhn, Elise Ferer, and Alisa Frohman all provided me with a shoulder to cry on in times of need and helped me map a path forward when I couldn't see one.

It took a village to raise me, and not just because I was a handful. Marianne Scanlon taught me to read by the time I was four, then brilliantly concocted a plan (with my mother) to put whiteout on my birth certificate to enroll me in kindergarten a year early. Patrick Scanlon held me in the palm of his hand as a baby, and together with Marianne and my mother raised me to be smart and empowered woman. Joann and Arthur Metcalf and Christopher "Daddy Chris" and Eva Mae "Mother Eve" McDaniel were the grandparents I cherished as a girl. Margo and Chuck Reeg, the late Debbie and Raul Escobedo, the Husners, the Starks, and countless other families comprised and sustained the wonderful neighborhood I grew up in, one that I will always call home. In more recent years, Uncle Drew and Carol Metcalf provided me with love and laughter on the East Coast—their kindness and generosity is unfathomable. Meanwhile, Nancy McDonald and Jeff Davis offer me much the same here on the West Coast, and for that I'm truly grateful. I have too many cousins to name, but I love each and every one of you to pieces.

My amazing mother is my guiding light, and deserves the most praise here. She always believed in me, always wanted the best for me, and always loved me more than anything in the world. Her love and support never faltered and continue to steer me in the right direction. This society is not kind to single mothers, especially those with few financial resources. This book is every bit as much her achievement as it is mine. My faults are my own, but whatever positive traits I have come from her—particularly resilience, warmth, and a love for animals. Before I forget: Gracie Dog, treats are on me if this book sells.

Finally, for all of my amazing students over the past few years, who now reside close by in Los Angeles, or far away in Namibia, the honor of teaching you (and learning from you) has always been mine.

Twists of Fate

Introduction

That coalitions form among members of Congress along shared interests is nothing new—such has been the case since the inception of the institution, and should be expected within legislative bodies. As a more recently established coalition, the Congressional Tri-Caucus—which includes the Congressional Black, Hispanic, and Asian Pacific American Caucuses—offers a decidedly different twist. While racial minorities in Congress have long sought substantive policy gains, the Tri-Caucus represents the first deliberately cross-cultural alliance designed for the specific purpose of exchanging ideas and promoting a solid voting bloc that leaves no racial minority group behind.

Officially convened in 2005, the votes of the members of the Tri-Caucus vary somewhat, but generally not enough to question their influence. With seventy to eighty House members present and voting in a given session, they exercise considerable input into and control over both legislation and legislative priorities within the Democratic Caucus. In so doing, these members effectively redirect a major party with a complicated history; although the Democratic Party is notable for broadly advocating principles of equality in the form of civil rights and equal rights since the 1960s, the deliberate omissions of minority concerns from the national agenda and the exacerbation of intergroup differences within the party apparatus plays heavily in the continued suppression of minority voices.

In part, this book examines the indirect interplay between Congress and the courts as a means to grapple with the idea of effective representation for marginalized communities—racial minorities in particular. That is, provisions of the Voting Rights Act (VRA) have been necessary but insufficient catalysts for change in the policymaking process of legislative bodies. In the early twenty-first century, numerous court cases on voting rights have been decided—many with a direct impact on the ability of members from and representing minority communities to successfully "influence" the policy process. I assess one particular aspect of the various voting rights outcomes, by asking: does the creation of *both* majority-minority and influence districts (which have a 30 to 50 percent minority voting age population) offer greater policy input for minority groups as a whole? If so, under what conditions does this improved input occur? The impetus here is to provide the reader with a better understanding of where support for civil rights can be found in the House of Representatives. These gains, particularly in terms of actual policy support for civil rights, are both direct and indirect byproducts of passage of the Voting Rights Act of 1965 (along with subsequent amendments and legal challenges), but in effect, they remain insufficient.

As such, this book picks up where certain others have left off, by focusing on the question: If civil rights support remains mixed at best, how have members of Congress from and representing racial minority groups changed their strategies of advocacy for civil rights? Perhaps even more ambitious, through elite interviewing I explore how these members' own attitudes have evolved toward a collective understanding of marginalization that extends beyond their personal racial backgrounds and now increasingly includes other racial groups, as well as groups that have been targets of systemic discrimination, such as women, children, the impoverished, and the lesbian, gay, bisexual, and transgender (LGBT) community.

An equally important aspect of this book is the changing dynamics of minority politics at the federal level, which have evolved considerably since the beginning of the twenty-first century. In the 1990s, racial group competition at the local level was the norm, and rarely would stories emerge about multiracial coalitions. To the contrary, the United States witnessed countless acts of intergroup conflict, particularly in states with significant minority populations such as California, Illinois, New York, and Texas. Most, though certainly not all, of this conflict took place at the local level.

Here I also emphasize that members of the House of Representatives, though they make policy at the federal level of government, essentially remain local politicians. Many congressional members from and representing communities of color are essentially delegates of the geographic districts that elected them, not unlike their white counterparts. To the extent that their constituents witness or participate in intergroup acrimony, elected officials are often limited in their ability to foster beneficial intergroup relations at home.

Despite racial tensions in their districts, many of these members have found that the political environment in Washington, DC varies greatly from the familiarity of home. Almost universally Democrats, members from and representing communities of color find the inner workings of Capitol Hill to be highly exclusive, not only as they attempt to navigate partisan politics, but also as they wind their way through the complex intricacies of seniority, committee assignments, and perhaps most prominently, fundraising.

So it follows that these members from and representing communities of color (1) conceive of "influence" in a markedly different way than the highest reaches of the judiciary, and (2) have adopted alternative strategies for success, reflecting a *linked political fate* that exists among these groups, as opposed to solely within each of them. That is, given the type of structural hurdles that largely go unaccounted for in judicial assessments, legislators from specific racial groups have adapted to their new congressional environment by building a unique multiracial coalition. This newfound coalition presents a twofold shift, in that it differs considerably both from the competitive approaches often espoused at the local level, and from the prior lack of interaction among racial minority groups at the federal level of the policy process.

Congressional lawmakers, state-level lawmakers, executive officials, and jurists have long debated, and chafed against, the means to achieve sufficient representation for minority communities across the country. Race-conscious redistricting strategies are but one attempt to address and provide for minority influence in the American political structure. With a long history rife with tactics devised to discourage minority participation and prevent adequate representation for marginal groups,[1] the United States government has more recently employed policies designed to enable racial minority groups to vote without obstruction and elect candidates who will voice their interests and needs in the deliberative bodies of democratic politics. Whether and how these needs will be sufficiently met remains subject to ongoing debate. In a majority rule system with a finite amount of resources, the needs of social groups outside a larger mainstream may systematically go unnoticed or unattended.

In addition to the successful achievement of substantive representation, much broader questions of fairness, equality, and opportunity arise out of the debates regarding the redistricting process and the best means to achieve quality representation for communities of color. While the Voting Rights Act has provided for greater numbers of minority representatives at all levels of government, does this mean that racial minorities now have more "influence" in the process, and is that influence enough to both undo detrimental policies and create substantive, beneficial change? Given specific structural and organizational constraints, such as majority party status and negative powers in the legislative process, what circumstances must be present for the US House of Representatives to better meet the needs of marginal groups? How do members of Congress garner influence in the legislative process, and have Congressional members from and representing marginal groups had difficulty gaining access to traditional avenues to influence?

The plan of my project here is fourfold: first, I conceptualize political influence and explore (from a theoretical standpoint) when and where lawmakers from and representing marginal groups are able to exert influence in the legislative arena. I specifically focus on hurdles that hinder their ability to successfully implement policy change, and I look for potential strategies to increase their influence in the process, despite the hurdles they might face. I direct my primary focus on more recently adopted strategies to secure beneficial policy outcomes. This goal requires the development of a conceptual understanding of political influence, borrowing from other scholars and researchers as well as providing an original presentation of the necessary components of political influence in contemporary times, and the circumstances that must be present for those representing marginal groups to garner influence in the process.

Second, I look at the political histories of people of color (particularly black, Latino, and Asian American) and American civil rights history to try and assess the gains and losses of political influence since the end of the Civil War, starting with the period of Reconstruction in the South. Historically, minorities have had more influence over political outcomes during different time periods, often corresponding with the willingness of governmental bodies to intervene and protect the rights of ethnic communities. When have these communities been able to exert influence in the political process, especially through the legislative branch? How has their ability to participate in the political process and elect candidates of their choice changed and grown in years past? Also, when have interracial coalitions flourished and how have they fared throughout the years?

Third, returning to the Voting Rights Act and the function of redistricting, I focus on the legislative behavior of congressional representatives, focusing specifically on the type of district they represent: majority-minority, influence, or white supermajority. In particular, given the assertions made both by elected officials and social scientists, I offer statistical analysis to better inform the debate. How does the voting behavior of those representing influence districts differ from those representing majority-minority districts and supermajority white districts? Using both quantitative and qualitative approaches, I aim to flesh out the variations in legislative voting behavior to account for the quality of representation that is afforded to minority constituents. I augment my numerical findings with quotes from interviews with members of Congress and redistricting experts to better understand the issues behind redistricting and the representation of marginal groups in Congress.

Fourth and finally, using forty-seven in-depth, confidential interviews with members of Congress from both parties and multiple racial backgrounds, I ask how legislators personally define and describe influence in the legislative process. What does it mean to have real influence in politics? How does one go about garnering and wielding influence? For members representing majority-minority districts, I ask specifically if they feel their experience has been impacted by their district status. For all members, I ask if they have difficulty navigating the racial politics of their districts, and if they see themselves as advocates for civil rights legislation in the House. I also ask each member about coalition-building in the House, and whether they feel that there is a linked political fate between racial minority constituencies, and inquire about the extent to which that linked political fate extends to other marginalized communities.

This research differs from prior published work in both approach and method. Congressional scholars who have focused on influence in the legislative process have not focused heavily on critical factors such as marginalized status. Unlike previous work done on the representation of minority groups that focuses on the race of the representative and the differences in legislative behavior (see Swain 1993; Whitby 1998; Canon 1999; Tate 2003), I also explore representation based on the type of district represented, paying considerable attention to the utility of interracial alliances and coalitional strategies in legislative behavior. The potential for alliances between black, Latino, and Asian American representatives in particular is rarely discussed in congressional research; but given the increasing diversity of the American population, it deserves much more attention from political scientists (notable exceptions to this general lack include Minta 2011; and Hero and Preuhs 2013). I also place much more weight on the opinions of actual members of Congress, by devoting considerable energy to conducting interviews and thus providing a more intimate perspective than quantitative analysis alone can provide. In a larger context, these answers provide a better understanding of the internal dynamics of Congress, what it means to have real influence in the process, and the implications that exist for marginalized communities trying to gain political power in a system that has historically excluded them and overlooked their policy needs.

WHY CARE ABOUT *INFLUENCE*?

Narrow definitions of influence and representation by the courts and others may have led political scientists to ask, if not the wrong questions,

then only a small part of the questions we need to ask in order to understand how representation and voice work in our democracy. Not enough
attention has been spent examining the dynamics of power in legislative
systems, and how members from and representing marginal groups may
be systematically shut out of various avenues typically utilized to gain
influence in the process. In many cases, this means that the groups that
most desperately need their policy concerns to be addressed are the least
likely to be recognized. In essence, members from and representing racial
minority groups often find themselves in a unique predicament: their
constituencies tend to be more economically disadvantaged than those
of their white counterparts, and they themselves experience marginalization during the process of policy formulation on Capitol Hill.

In Supreme Court debates over the maximization of influence districts
in addition to majority-minority districts, multiple types of influence
were conflated. The first type of influence concerns the electoral ability
minority groups have to determine their representative. That is, will racial
minority communities in a geographic district have the wherewithal to
elect a representative of their choice? Second, to what degree will the substantive interests of those communities be represented and/or realized in
a given legislative body? Finally, there remains the question of how successful those representatives will be in achieving policy outcomes. That
is, how much influence do those individual representatives who argue on
behalf of the substantive interests of their constituents have in successfully passing legislation? It is important to differentiate between these distinct forms of influence, which I refer to as *electoral influence, constituent
policy influence*, and *representative policy influence*, as they play different
roles in the process of democracy, and they are at the heart of the debate
over minority representation in a majority rule system of government.

Electoral influence refers specifically to the ability of a voter or group of
voters to influence the outcome of a given election. Here the link between
influence and voter participation is best explained. Voter turnout rates
remain integral to electoral success, and are often impacted by campaign
donations and group endorsements. Many empirical questions fall into
the realm of electoral influence: Will a voter or group of voters achieve

descriptive representation? Will that voter or group be able to elect a
person from their own party?

Constituent policy influence occurs after an election. This term refers
to the ability that a voter or group has to influence the political behavior
of an elected official, and to persuade that legislator to vote the constituent's or group's preferences on a given policy or set of policies, initiate
policy on their behalf, or provide other types of support as they deem
necessary. Will an elected official recognize and respond to (a) the substantive needs of that individual or group and/or (b) the policy preferences of that individual or group? Will that official take a leadership role
in obtaining these objectives? Will the individuals or groups have access
to their elected official, and opportunities to voice their concerns?

Representative policy influence provides the final connection in the
continuum. Broadly, this phrase refers to the amount of influence a single
elected official wields in the overall legislative process. Whether that official actually has the wherewithal not only to voice the concerns of his
or her constituents, but also to persuade his or her colleagues to provide
support as well, is a very powerful form of influence that is exceedingly
difficult to quantify and is often overlooked by the courts. Although most
members of Congress serving in the House of Representatives have a
vote,[2] the distribution of political capital within the chamber is not universal. Does a member of Congress have enough allies to create the substantive change to meet the needs of his or her constituents? How would a
representative go about obtaining the allies necessary to successfully pass
policy initiatives through the legislature?

A strong relationship exists between the first two types of influence.
Intuitively, electoral influence (as defined through voter turnout) has an
effect on policy. In an ideal world, citizens turn out to the polls and vote
for the candidate they believe will best support their substantive policy
needs and voice their concerns. Candidates can only serve as policymak-
ers with the electoral support of their constituents. Candidates elected
by their constituents are assumed to have the power to directly influence
legislative policy outcomes.

In turn, constituent policy influence also has an effect on electoral support and general district-level politics. Whether constituents are compelled to vote may reflect the policy record of the incumbent. The policy decisions made by a legislator, and that legislator's willingness to address the substantive needs and concerns of an individual or group, may encourage or discourage electoral support back at home in the district. That is, the ability of a group to exert policy influence (conveyed through responsiveness to concerns and legislative behavior) may affect the overall desire to participate in the political system.

While the first two types of influence have an effect on the other, they are not one and the same. Moreover, neither guarantees that a representative will have the necessary political capital to meet the substantive needs of his or her constituents. Constituent policy influence does not necessarily follow electoral influence. While an individual or group may choose to support a candidate with their vote, the candidate, if elected, is not required to meet the policy needs and interests of that individual or group. Hall (1996) makes it clear that the assumption that, once elected, an agent will participate in legislative decisions is unsubstantiated. Similarly, if the elected official does not pursue the substantive needs of an individual or group, he or she will not necessarily lose electoral support from those whose interests they have neglected. In some instances, a group may choose to vote for that elected official because the alternative is much farther from their perceived interests and preferences. On other occasions, an incumbent legislator may be running unopposed, and constituents may not have the opportunity to vote him or her out of office. As such, the alternative is to not participate in the voting process at all.

An ongoing debate exists concerning the achievement of fairness for groups that have been historically excluded from dominant institutions and their resources. For some, to achieve "fairness" (Guinier 1994), one necessary relationship between the first two types of influence is accountability. Principally, an elected official who is not responsive to the substantive needs and requests of constituents can lose crucial electoral support, and consequently be replaced by a challenger. But to have a representative who voices the needs and interests of a marginal group, and is held accountable by that group, does not mean that the needs of that group will ever be fulfilled. To the contrary, it is quite possible that those needs go systematically unaddressed.

This point must be emphasized. I argue that electoral influence and constituent policy influence are components of a fair democracy, but neither one, together or alone, can bring about actual policy change in a given legislature. In contemporary US politics, many marginal groups lack representative policy influence. Is it just or fair that the needs of a marginal group remain completely neglected or only minimally dealt with because the group lacks the size in population necessary to gain a critical mass? Does that lack of recognition by the mainstream only further entrench their marginal status?

VOTING RIGHTS HISTORY AND INCREASED INFLUENCE

A central focus of the past debate concerning racial minorities and political power has been inclusion, rather than the amount of influence or power necessary to produce substantive change. In most historical cases, minorities had little, if any, voice or input in federal policy. To the contrary, the direction of the nation was subject to the preferences and opinions of those in charge: mainly economically privileged, white males. Inclusion of minorities, manifested through federal statute with an emphasis on electoral influence, has been obtained through changes in redistricting policies and the achievement of descriptive representation. This section offers a brief summation of that history.

The Voting Rights Act of 1965 has been enormously successful in providing blacks and other minority groups with greater impact on government, both by securing their right to vote, and by establishing goals for continued inclusion. Indeed, there was considerable improvement to be made. By 1960, following the dismal failures of the Fifteenth Amendment and Reconstruction, less than one in four blacks had access to the franchise, and the consequent ability to elect representatives of their choice

(Sitkoff 1993). Despite vigilant opposition, most commonly in the form of Southern white resistance, passage of the VRA led to monumental changes in the racial makeup of legislative bodies across the country, as well as those who cast their ballots in support of those changes.

While Reconstruction efforts in the late 1860s and early 1870s gave way to tremendous successes in black participation on multiple levels, the gains were short-lived. In 1872, well over 300 blacks were elected to office, mostly in the South, but the Compromise of 1876 provided tacit consent to extreme forms of political exclusion in tandem with brutal violence and systematic oppression. Nearly a decade later, black elected officials were virtually nonexistent (Davidson 1992). Moreover, minority political participation took a swift dive, with Southern states revising their constitutions to exclude black voting at all levels.

To further ensure the exclusion of blacks, innumerable measures were put in place to prevent all types of interracial relationships and curtail the possibility of white support for black struggles and the growth of populism. The emergence of Jim Crow allowed for and perpetuated a racial hierarchy and vicious caste system designed to prevent alliances that would threaten Southern financial structures as well as the governments that kept them in place. The federal government was well aware of these procedures, yet turned a blind eye to the injustice.

Many of the discriminatory practices would continue throughout the next eighty years, with limited gains achieved most notably by the National Association for the Advancement of Colored People (NAACP). During the first half of the twentieth century, the NAACP would successfully challenge white primaries (*Smith v. Allwright*, 1944), unequal pay for teachers (*Mills v. the Board of Education of Anne Arundel County*, 1939),[3] and separate but equal provisions that allowed segregation in schooling (*Brown v. Board of Education in Topeka*, 1954). In 1960, in the case of *Gomillion v. Lightfoot*, the Supreme Court declared unconstitutional a law by which the boundaries of Tuskegee were drawn by the all-white legislature so that they only included five of the more than four hundred black residents.

Most of these events took place during the Civil Rights Movement, a period of heightened civil rights advocacy largely focused on the treatment

of African Americans in the South, but also extending to blacks in the
Northern and Western regions of the country. The movement, though
primarily focused on blacks, would increasingly include all racial minorities, as burgeoning anti-discrimination activism emerged in Latino, Asian
Pacific Islander, and Native American enclaves throughout the nation.
From bus boycotts to student sit-ins, the coordination of activism, combined with nationwide cries for racial justice, bolstered the momentum of
the movement in multiple arenas, particularly those social and political.

The staunch persistence of political exclusion, most notably in the
South, continued well into the 1960s. Voter registration drives conducted
in the Southern states of Alabama, Mississippi, and Louisiana repeatedly led to bloodshed, with the most memorable incident being "Bloody
Sunday" on March 7, 1965, where nearly one hundred peaceful demon-
strators were injured by state troopers in Alabama while marching to
the state capitol. By the spring of 1965, President Johnson presented his
voting rights bill to Congress. It passed through both houses that following August, with divisions drawn not along partisan lines, but along
regional lines. Northern members of Congress voted overwhelmingly in
favor, while Southerners overwhelmingly voted against (Davidson 1992).

The Voting Rights Act, with major provisions including Sections 2 and
5, did much to reverse the trends of political exclusion, placing the power
of direct action and enforcement within the executive branch of the federal
government. Discriminatory procedures such as literacy tests, grandfather
clauses, and other forms of racially motivated disenfranchisement were
banned in states and counties where less than 50 percent of the voting age
population was registered or had actually voted in the 1964 presidential
election—a ban that was extended nationwide a few years later. States were
strictly forbidden from denying the right to vote on the basis of race, and
federal approval of planned changes in state voting procedures for those
states that had systematically discriminated against ethnic minorities
was mandated. Notable among these was the requirement that proposed
changes in electoral policies, including geographically-drawn district lines,
would only be permissible after federal jurists confirmed that they would
not deny or abridge the right to vote in either purpose or effect.

Since passage of the VRA, a lion's share of the pragmatic debate over voting rights in the United States has centered on minority vote dilution, and the best means to ensure that ethnic groups are not systematically excluded from the political process. Vote dilution remains an integral concern in redistricting procedures, with oversight and enforcement by the federal government officially coded into law. Defined as "a process where election laws or practices, either singly or in concert, combined with systematic bloc voting among an identifiable majority group to diminish or cancel the voting strength of at least one minority group,"[4] multiple approaches to the prevention of vote dilution have emerged—most prominently the maximization of majority-minority districts in legislative bodies.

The evolution of redistricting practices and the consequent number of minority elected officials has varied significantly over the years, due in part to changes in the wording of the Voting Rights Act, but also due to changes in interpretation of the Act. Congress introduced significant amendments to the Act in 1970, 1975, and 1982 that further expanded its scope. Court decisions worked in tandem with these amendments to reinforce the adopted changes and set precedents for future challenges, while agency support for enforcement provided more impetus for state compliance.

In particular, the amendments to the Voting Rights Act of 1975 and 1982 significantly broadened the mandate of the original legislation. In 1975, the legislature ordered that language minorities also be protected from discrimination and dilution. Following lengthy testimony by Latinos, Asian Americans, and Native Americans, Congress determined that citizens of certain ethnic groups, especially newly naturalized citizens, were not sufficiently fluent in English to understand complicated election materials. The 1975 amendments added language minority status to Section 2, forbidding any jurisdiction from enacting an election law that denied or abridged voting rights on the basis of language, permanently placing language minorities as a protected class.

In 1982, as amended, Section 2 rendered any state law that had the effect (not merely the purpose or intent) of minority vote dilution illegal. In explicit language, the Voting Rights Act was reworded so "that proof of discriminatory results was sufficient to substantiate a claim of dilution" and was renewed for twenty-five years (Davidson 1992). A results-based test was also brought in to further encourage minority representation. And notably, Section 5 of the VRA, which included the non-retrogression clause and the requirement for preclearance by the Attorney General's Office or the District Court for the District of Columbia, was extended.

Court decisions also played a substantial role in the shaping of the Voting Rights Act, though at times they were sharply divided. In 1973, the *White v. Regester* decision reflected the Supreme Court's belief that the minimal number of black legislators in the congressional districts around and including San Antonio and Dallas was the result of unconstitutional vote dilution practices in Texas, though no definitive criteria were put forth to determine the existence of vote dilution. In contrast, in the *City of Mobile v. Bolden* (1980), the Supreme Court ruled that plaintiffs must prove the purpose or intent of discrimination in situations where vote dilution is taking place, not merely the result of such discrimination.

After the 1982 amendments to the Voting Rights Act passed, the Court took a different approach. The 1986 ruling in *Thornburg v. Gingles* was widely interpreted to require that states create majority-minority districts wherever possible. This decision presented a significant departure from the prior standard that required "non-retrogression," manifested as the preservation of existing minority districts. Moreover, the Court put forth specific guidelines and criteria for determining the presence of vote dilution. The Department of Justice further reinforced the legislation and court opinions, declaring that it would not preclear laws that violated Section 2. Non-retrogressive policies were no longer sufficient.

By 1990, redistricting scholars learned a new rule of thumb: majority black or Hispanic districts should be created wherever possible (Congressional Quarterly 1993). This plan became the benchmark for contemporary legislative redistricting procedures. The maximization of majority-minority districts resulted in a sizable increase in the number of minorities in legislative bodies at all levels nationwide, with the freshman congressional class of 1992 including sixteen blacks and eight Hispanics. These districts were drawn in addition to the preexisting majority-minority districts, which were preserved under the non-retrogression standard.

Since passage of the 1982 amendments, most of the activity related to redistricting practices has occurred in the judicial branch, with the exception of amendments passed through legislation in 1992 extending the requirement of bilingual voting materials. In July 2006, both houses of Congress voted to extend the Voting Rights Act by a wide margin. Later that month, the bill was signed into law by President George W. Bush.

MARGINAL GROUPS, RACE, AND REPRESENTATION

The existence of marginal groups is seldom questioned, though the precise degree of the marginalization that they suffer can be contentious. In most societies, certain groups have suffered systematic discrimination, where they are repeatedly denied access to resources and offered only limited levels of participation in the dominant institutions of that culture. While they need not be entirely powerless, these groups still remain outside of a mainstream, perceived as "others" in a civilization where they are on the outside, looking in.

In her book *The Boundaries of Blackness* (1999), Cathy Cohen provides the following:

> I assume that a group is marginal to the extent that its members have historically been and continue to be denied access to dominant decision-making processes and institutions; stigmatized by their identification; isolated or segregated; and generally excluded from control over the resources that shape the quality of their lives. (24)

From there, Cohen delineates a framework of marginalization, in which she puts forth three major principles that aid the understanding of the political behavior of marginal groups:

1. A focus on the history of power relations and oppression under which groups evolve;
2. Centrality of the indigenous structure of marginal communities in understanding their political choices; and

3. The recognition that strategies of marginalization are not
   static but evolve over time, responding in part dialectically to
   the resistance of marginal group members. (25)

These three principles highlight a special need to examine context when
analyzing the political behavior of marginalized communities and their
representatives. First, historical experiences of exclusion, inequality, and
oppression inevitably affect the present and future political choices of
these groups and actors within the groups. Reactions to certain issues
may be the result of prior experiences, during which views about the
world and the self formed. Second, the relationship and structures that
exist within a marginal group must be carefully considered. Indigenous
advocacy groups and other institutions within a given community may
impact choices made by their representatives. Finally, marginalization
occurs to different degrees and manifests in multiple ways. To best understand the behavior of marginal groups, it is important to understand
the variations of exclusion and oppression they have experienced.

Marginalization occurs systematically and efficiently, often precisely
because it is without observed intent. Oppression, argues Iris Marion
Young (1990), comes as a consequence of

unconscious assumptions and reactions of well-meaning people in
ordinary interactions, media and cultural stereotypes, and structural
features of bureaucratic hierarchies and market mechanisms—in
short, the normal processes of everyday life. (41)

Young's "structural features" pervade American politics, and the position of blacks and other racial minority groups remains tenuous in a
two-party system. While candidates and elected officials may ostensibly
respond to the needs of all voters, party competition is often central-
ized around racially conservative white voters, which can have dire consequences for African Americans and other minority groups. Partisan
strategies for electoral success almost necessarily require competition
over white swing voters, and a consequent appearance of distance from

African Americans, leaving blacks with unappealing choices, and bleak hopes for policy change in the future (Frymer 1999).

> If a nation is divided by race, with one group indelibly in the minority, the two party system places the center of conflict and attention around the majority group. In turn, the minority group becomes further demobilized and, in the process, loses most semblances of representation in American politics. (Frymer 1999, 139)

Meanwhile, the often unfulfilled promises of pluralism have lessened the chances for blacks and other racial minorities to obtain political influence in US legislative politics. While theories suggest that political coalitions will shift and fluctuate across various issues, the increased polarization in current politics repeatedly prevents this goal (Hansen 2005). The lack of shifting coalitions (current legislative coalitions seem notably embedded), combined with the concentration of certain groups in political and economic elites, places racial minorities at a structural disadvantage.

As I explore the dynamics of influence across the political spectrum, I acknowledge that both the quantity and quality of representation for racial minorities has improved in recent years, providing benefits in various forms. Since the passage of the Voting Rights Act, the racial compositions of legislatures across the country have changed to better reflect the racial and ethnic diversity of the United States through descriptive, substantive, and symbolic means.

According to Pitkin (1967), *descriptive representation* refers to instances where a representative has the same descriptive attributes as his or her constituency, including but not limited to racial background, gender, or sexual orientation. A shared social or demographic characteristic between the representative and the constituent provides the foundation for one to descriptively represent one's constituency. *Substantive representation* generally refers to voting for, or even initiating various pieces of, substantive policy legislation that reflect the needs of the community represented. That is, a representative must help constituents to realize their political needs or preferences, whatever they may be. *Symbolic representation* occurs when an elected official offers symbolic acts, such as renaming streets, parks, and schools in the district. The symbolism need not include substantive policy changes, nor does it dramatically alter the lives of constituents, but it may have the benefit of boosting morale within a given geographic area or district. In each way, representation for racial minority groups has increased tremendously.

A debate has surfaced, however, concerning the benefits derived from the various forms of representation—especially descriptive representation for racial minorities in the United States. While most scholars agree that substantive representation tremendously benefits constituents, descriptive and symbolic representation receive more scrutiny. Swain takes aim at descriptive representation, claiming that elected officials need not be black to represent the political needs and interests of black constituents (1993). Rather, the push for descriptive representation in black communities actively undermines their substantive representation in Congress, while partisan affiliation best determines the quality of substantive representation for blacks.

The Supreme Court, in the *Georgia v. Ashcroft* (2003) decision encouraging the creation of influence districts, cited Swain and offered the following in regards to descriptive and substantive representation:

> Section 5 leaves room for States to use these types of influence and coalitional districts. Indeed, the State's choice ultimately may rest on a political choice of whether substantive or descriptive representation is preferable. The State may choose, consistent with Section 5, that it is better to risk having fewer minority representatives in order to achieve greater overall representation of a minority group by increasing the number of representatives sympathetic to the interests of minority voters. (19)

The potential benefits of descriptive representation have certainly been considered. Katherine Tate (2003) argues that the racial composition of the legislative branch correlates with the political representation of blacks. Most Americans, regardless of race, place a strong value on descriptive representation, and blacks are not the least among them. Tate finds black legislators are much more likely to have shared experiences with their black constituents than are white legislators. They are less wealthy than their white counterparts. Black female legislators are much more likely to have been single parents at some point in their lives than white female legislators. Black legislators were also more likely to report having experienced racial discrimination (Tate 2003). Her findings suggest that black members of Congress remain equally successful in bill attainment when compared to white counterparts, and that the policies they propose are not lacking in substance.

> Black legislators provide Black constituents with the greatest amount of "symbolic" representation, but also initiate and participate in providing their black constituents with policies of substance, namely those that distribute or redistribute tangible public goods. (97)

Meanwhile, David Lublin finds that the racial composition of a district directly relates to the roll-call voting patterns of the Representative. In both parties, legislators are generally unresponsive to blacks in their districts when blacks comprise less than 40 percent of the voting age population (1997).

While these prior studies provide insight through both their methods and outcomes, there remains an absence of work on collaboration among representatives of marginal groups, particularly those that are deliberately multiracial. What little research exists that ties black and Latino congressional efforts together still misses certain key components: namely, the intentionality of their collaborations; the strength of the relationships they have forged; and the inclusion of the Congressional Asian Pacific American Caucus. That is, while some scholars acknowledge that black and Latino lawmakers are much more likely to advocate on behalf of black and Latino interests in Congress (Minta 2011), they do not expand upon the deliberately concerted behavior of the members of the Tri-Caucus, nor do they carefully consider the contributions that members from Asian Pacific Islander backgrounds might offer.

Similarly, Hero and Preuhs find that black-Latino relations are characterized by nonconflict, but also by independence (2013). On this point and a few others, I take issue, and argue that in fact the members of the Congressional Black, Hispanic, and Asian Pacific American Caucuses have become intentional collaborators since 2005, to the point where Democratic leadership in the House of Representatives no longer asks, "What does the Black Caucus want?" Rather, the prominent question has become, "What does the Tri-Caucus want?"

Finally, and perhaps most importantly, unlike the work of Minta (2011) and Hero and Preuhs (2013), I look at more recent voting behavior by members of the Congressional Tri-Caucus. Both of these prior works rely heavily on data prior to the 108th Congress (2003–2004), and only Hero and Preuhs explore voting behavior during the 108th Congress. The Congressional Tri-Caucus was not established as a legislative service organization until 2005. I use the voting records from the 108th and 109th Congresses (2003–2006), which paint a somewhat different picture of multiracial collaboration, and I interview members of Congress with the intent not only of describing the dynamics through statistical evidence, but also of fleshing out the back story with the words of the members themselves.

QUESTIONS

A wide range of research questions arose both prior to and during the field-work phase of this project. Initially, my focus was solely upon the two types of policy influence I explained earlier—constituent and representative—discerning each through both statistical analysis and primary research from interviews with members of Congress. But while conducting my in-depth, semi-structured interviews with forty-seven members of the US House of Representatives, and exploring my theory of linked political fate, many of the racial minority members themselves brought up the positive benefits of their relatively new coalition, the Congressional Tri-Caucus. For many, it seemed, the formation of the Tri-Caucus remained a source of both pride in the success of the endeavor and hope for the future.

Moreover, through interviews with the executive directors of each of the three caucuses, I learned that daily communication had become standard, even if orchestrated events remained less frequent.

In analyzing constituent policy influence, where representative behavior directly reflects the perceived needs of their constituents, I explore the receptivity of legislators to voting on behalf of or initiating changes that are pro-"civil rights" and favorable to disadvantaged or marginalized groups as a whole. In contrast with the *Georgia v. Ashcroft* Supreme Court decision, I expect support for civil rights (broadly defined) will be substantially higher in majority-minority districts than in either influence districts or in districts with white supermajorities. Substantial research has been conducted to examine the racial gap in policy preferences between black and white Americans. Preferences, opinions, and attitudes vary significantly along the lines of race (Kinder and Sanders 1996; Schuman et al. 1997; Dawson and Popoff 2004), with white Americans holding more conservative views toward civil rights and social welfare policies. Meanwhile, Gilens (1999) finds that public opinion surrounding anti-poverty policies is highly influenced by racial politics. Specifically, he finds that negative racial stereotypes about blacks determine white America's support (or lack thereof) for welfare. The more that race-neutral anti-poverty policies (such as Temporary Aid to Needy Families and food stamp programs) *appear* to benefit racial minorities, specifically blacks, the more likely it is that whites will oppose them.

I also question whether representatives of influence districts will be less likely than members of majority-minority districts to support policies seen to benefit marginalized ethnic groups: namely traditional civil rights issues and progressive social welfare policies. No matter their preference, a favorable vote, let alone support through sponsorship or co-sponsorship, might jeopardize their chances for reelection in a predominantly white district and leave them vulnerable to more conservative opposition.

I pay specific attention to the relationships between members of the Tri-Caucus, including the Congressional Black Caucus, Congressional Hispanic Caucus, and Congressional Asian Pacific American Caucus. Are they motivated by rationales more specific to their marginal status? How do they navigate the system? Do they develop strategies that differ from those of their white counterparts? Given their marginal status and the potentially corresponding status of their districts, what did they hope to achieve with the Tri-Caucus? That is, if the formation of the Congressional Tri-Caucus occurred as a specific strategy to increase their influence in the policy process, how would it do so? What would that look like?

METHODOLOGY AND DATA

This project requires both qualitative and quantitative approaches to flesh out the nuances of influence in the policy process: both constituent policy influence and representative policy influence. I ask multiple questions designed to illuminate various forms of policy influence in the political process. Moreover, I pay special attention to the unique circumstances of marginalized communities as they and their representatives work within the system and navigate the various political institutions, particularly Congress. Using historical analysis, roll-call analysis, and elite interviewing, I explore the conditions that have been necessary throughout United States history for marginal groups to gain political influence, the variations in levels of support for civil rights legislation by district type, and the dynamics of coalitional politics among members of Congress, especially those representing districts with large populations of marginal groups.

To better understand constituent policy influence, I examine levels of support for civil rights legislation. The term "civil rights" can be easily misconstrued, as many varying definitions and designs of civil rights exist. For this project, I rely on the Leadership Conference on Civil Rights to determine whether a policy should be categorized as civil rights legislation. Using quantitative methods, I contrast the behavior of representatives of influence districts with other types of districts in two separate categories: (1) traditional civil rights issues and anti-discrimination policies, such as fair housing and equal employment opportunity; and (2) contemporary social welfare issues such as AIDS funding and healthcare for the economically disadvantaged, food stamps, and other welfare-related policies.

Certain dynamics should be mentioned here. First, my use of Leadership Conference on Civil Rights (LCCR) scores as a measure of civil rights may come into question because of the inclusive nature of the scores. The Leadership Conference on Civil Rights continues to serve as an umbrella organization for a number of marginal groups, including racial minorities, women, and the LGBT community. There has been a consistent pull since the 1960s to limit the discourse on civil rights to issues *universally* affecting African Americans and other racial minority groups. This position, however, seems to contradict the goals of most civil rights organizations. For example, as Strolovitch wrote in 2006,

> By announcing broad policy agendas and a determination to speak for *all* members of a given constituency, advocacy organizations claim implicitly to speak for less privileged members of these groups. (898, emphasis mine)

In making this argument, I underscore the importance of not allowing disadvantaged subgroups of racial minority populations to be marginalized by the larger civil rights community. Moreover, a comprehensive model of marginalization should inform our understanding of group dominance and power in American society, and compel us to include groups and subgroups that decades ago may have not fallen into traditional categories of civil rights. A comprehensive model of marginalization is one that extends well beyond issues of race or the privileged subgroups within a marginalized community. For instance, a more contemporary model of marginalization would be class-, gender-, and orientation-inclusive, and would be focused on universal equality, not merely gains for a few select groups or subgroups of the population.

Second, there exists a need to underscore variation in the preferences of marginal groups and their representatives. In the interviews I conducted, I specifically questioned members about their voting behavior relative to their perceived understanding of their constituents' policy preferences. I understood that there is a wide range of policy attitudes within marginalized groups, and the underlying foundations of those attitudes have been reflected in research on black political theory (Dawson 2001). While controlling for nuances of public opinion at the district level is virtually impossible, I carefully considered it during my legislative interviews.

More generally, to better understand dynamics that quantitative research may not—and in certain instances cannot—reflect, I use historical data and elite interviews. For the historical account of voting rights and policy influence in retrospect, I rely upon collections from the library at Harvard University and the civil rights collection at the Library of Congress in Washington, DC. Personal accounts, acquired through interviews with members of Congress, their staff, and experts on voting rights and redistricting policies are used to share perspectives on the special characteristics of specific districts, and the difficulties (or lack thereof) inherent in representing diverse communities.

To gauge representative policy influence, primary sources allow us better insight into the positions of elected officials when deciding their level of support or opposition for different types of legislation. How would they describe political influence, both for individual legislators, as well as constituent interest groups? How do they go about coalition-building with their colleagues? Are there specific issues on which constituents in their districts seem divided? How do they resolve issues of competing preferences in the district? How does that complicate the ability of elected officials to represent the interests of their constituents? What are their preferences regarding redistricting? Do they consider themselves advocates for civil rights? Do they feel that the racial demographics of their district influence their policy decisions? If they represent groups at risk, how should those groups go about gaining more influence in the legislative process?

OUTLINE AND OVERVIEW

In this project, I examine policy influence, representation, and the ability of marginal groups to navigate the federal legislative arena. What does it mean to have influence? How and when has it been obtained by groups traditionally shut out from the political system? Is there adequate opportunity to achieve representation for minority needs and concerns, or have minority communities and minority members been excluded from traditional avenues of influence in legislative politics?

In chapter 2, I provide a theoretical understanding of influence. How is "influence" defined generally? How has the Supreme Court defined influence (with regards to redistricting) and is that definition sufficient? What does it mean for marginal groups (racial minorities in this case) to have "influence" in a system where only the candidate with the greatest number of votes reaches office and initiates subsequent policies and reforms? It has been argued that "influence districts" is a misnomer, especially given the American majority rule system of government. To exercise influence, marginalized communities may be forced to rely upon their ability to persuade a larger mainstream to join their cause—an option that seems tricky at best.

I also explore the difference between the policy *preferences* and policy *interests* of marginalized groups, where the political preferences of individuals are not necessarily in their best interests. In representing the interests of marginalized groups in Congress, a member of the House of Representatives may opt to vote counter to his or her perceived district preferences, precisely because it is in the best interests of those he or she represents. While many pieces of legislation are noncontroversial, some of the most polarizing national issues center on forms of targeted discrimination, and may or may not be overwhelmingly supported within a marginal group.

Finally, building upon Dawson's work on linked fate, I question whether the perceived linked fate that exists *within* certain marginalized groups[5] exists *among* these groups in the political realm, and then go on to develop a theory of *linked political fate*. That is, the success of individual racial groups can be directly related to each other. When a universal call for equality of all marginal groups is collectively advocated across the board, it may very well serve the best interests of each marginalized group individually. Thus, representatives may actually represent the best interests of their constituents without necessarily voting along the lines of their policy preferences. In other words, the interests of groups such as women, the LGBT community, the disabled, or the elderly, for example, not only overlap with, but also are inextricably linked to, the interests of racial minorities in the United States.

Chapter 3 focuses on the history of African American and other ethnic group attempts to gain influence in the federal electoral and legislative processes. In part, this chapter provides a history of voting rights and changes in the racial makeup of the voting populace, but it also offers a history of descriptive representation, where the number of black representatives has increased significantly since passage of the Fifteenth Amendment, and where Latinos have had a prominent role in politics in the Southwest for more than a century. Finally, it includes a recent history of policy influence, which consists of a summarizing look at when "civil rights" legislation has been passed by Congress.

Chapter 4 explores minority policy influence from a quantitative approach. First, I provide a more thorough description of the *Georgia v. Ashcroft* case. Then I ask, how responsive are representatives to the policy interests of minority constituents through support for "civil rights" legislation? Does the legislative behavior of representatives in influence districts vary considerably from those representing majority-minority districts and supermajority white districts? Using tobit regression analysis, I analyze the voting behavior on civil rights legislation that went to floor votes during the 108th and 109th Congresses. I address the issue of legislative support for civil rights policies, and the degree of support for both types of civil rights legislation (traditional civil rights policy and social welfare initiatives), and compare and contrast member behavior of influence districts with member behavior from non-influence districts. When and where do the members diverge in their voting behavior?

Chapter 5 uses interviews and primary sources to reexamine the issues of policy influence in a qualitative fashion. Quantitative analysis provides an overview of trends in voting behavior among representatives of influence and other types of districts, but it offers little insight into the inner workings of legislative activity. Under what conditions do constituent groups wield influence over members of Congress? Under what circumstances do those members wield influence over their colleagues on the Hill? I ask whether they believe their policy decisions are impacted by the dynamics of the district they represent. If so, how so? How precisely do they try to reflect their constituents' policy preferences? When and where do they opt to go against the preferences of their constituents, and how important is coalition-building in Washington?

Finally, Chapter 6 concludes with an assessment of the results of both the quantitative research of Chapter 4 and the qualitative research of Chapter 5. Is there constituent policy influence in influence districts? How does this match up with the interview responses members of Congress offer in Chapter 5? I also return to the broader question of influence and minority political power. A number of hurdles are in place preventing political influence (both electoral and policy) in communities of color. How else can influence be conceptualized? Will the current geographic district model ever allow minorities to truly garner and wield influence in the American political system? Finally, and most importantly, where does this dynamic leave members of marginal groups whose needs are systematically overlooked?

Marginalization, Linked Fate, and Coalitional Politics

A single interest has only rarely proven sufficient to generate a major change in legislative institutions. Instead intersections among multiple interests typically drive individual changes and the process of institutional development more generally.

—SCHICKLER 2001, 12

Whether it is used to describe an individual citizen, a group of citizens, or a policymaker looking to garner or wield influence through the legislative process, the notion of influence is considerable and complex. One must ask, what is required for an individual or group to be able to influence outcomes? What are the rules of the institution that govern access to influence? Further, when do legislators choose to cast votes based solely on constituency preferences, when do they vote their own personal preferences, and when do they use political calculus and coalition-building to increase their influence in the legislative body?

In the previous chapter, I introduced three separate types of influence in the legislative process, and the need to consider manifestations of marginalization both for communities of color, and for elected officials from and representing communities of color. In this chapter, I explore marginalization as it occurs during various stages of the legislative process, with particular attention to two types of influence—*constituent policy influence* and *representative policy influence*—with the hope of fleshing out a broader understanding of how dynamics of power manifest in our contemporary political system. I pay more attention to the two types of policy influence, leaving out electoral influence, because the intricacies of policy influence have received less consideration in research on racial minorities in the American political sphere than has electoral research. Though I utilize some of the literature in the field of political science,[1] most prominently Dawson's theory of linked fate (1994), Schickler's work on institutional change (2001), and Cohen's analysis of marginalization and public policy (1999), this chapter is not meant to be a comprehensive review of previous research.

Rather, this chapter presents a discussion of some of the circumstances that determine power and influence in Congress,[2] combined with an analysis of the unique position of members from and representing marginal groups as they attempt to improve the conditions of their constituents. In particular, I highlight the broad dynamics of status and marginalization and how they manifest in the political process, the utility of coalitional politics for racial minority groups, the advanced levels of mobilization necessary for constituent influence, and the politics and principles that play a role in legislative decision-making.

Marginalized communities (that is, groups that have been systematically excluded and oppressed by a dominant mainstream) have a unique position in the playing field of legislative politics because, although they often have shared interests and needs, they seldom have the requisite number of representatives necessary to influence policy outcomes without coalitional support. Using Cohen's framework of marginalization,[3] I ask whether members of marginalized communities, such as African Americans and Latinos, have an experience that is noticeably different from their white counterparts in garnering and wielding political influence as elected officials.[4] How does the status of either being a member of a marginalized group or representing a district comprised largely of marginalized constituents affect one's ability to garner legislative influence?

Finally, I address the relationship *between* marginalized communities, in contrast to the relationship they have with dominant political institutions as a whole. In the world of legislative politics, coalition-building is the tool of all groups as they attempt to produce change. In this chapter, I theorize about lateral interactions between various groups and I argue that a *linked political fate* among marginalized groups is often recognized and utilized in legislative politics. This linked fate does not exist solely within a particular group, but exists as a reality for a collective of groups, such as African Americans, Latinos, Asian Pacific Americans, women, and the LGBT community, who all seek to gain influence in the process. In turn, this circumstance results in a broad-based, liberal coalition that can more successfully create substantive policy change.

For this project, the experiences of groups that have been consistently excluded from power structures in America are not assumed to be the same. These marginalized groups have different histories, some in the United States and some abroad. Even within these groups, the experiences of individuals will be varied and distinctive. Despite the external and internal variation within and among racial minority groups, I seek to identify patterns and trends that members of these groups more commonly experience, having been traditionally marginalized through social, economic, and political exclusion. Though these shared experiences may be witnessed and understood to different degrees, their exploration may better illuminate the political ways and means of racially marginal groups as they, along with other marginalized communities, navigate the legislative process.

In *The Boundaries of Blackness* (1999), Cathy Cohen provides a framework for understanding the differing experiences of marginality across and within black America. With that work as an integral tool, I ask *how* and *when* does marginalization occur in the various stages of the legislative process, and what is the course that those from and representing marginal groups must take to gain influence in the process? I focus on the shared experiences among racially marginal groups and the consequent strategies and coping mechanisms among legislators from and representing racially marginalized communities. I reconsider partisan theories of legislative behavior that do not reflect variations that exist for legislators representing marginal groups. I also contemplate representation styles, and how the demographic composition of a district may affect the leadership of an elected official. Given the constraints of a two-party, winner-take-all system, I consider the ability of those representing marginal communities to obtain the votes necessary to create substantive policy change.

Institutional change remains a lofty goal in American politics, one that occurs rarely and not without exceptional vigor put forth by broad coalitions (Schickler 2001). Today we see alliances forming in Congress that cross many boundaries, the most prominent such boundary being race. Relatively little research in political science has been conducted on the impact that race has made, and continues to make, on policy formulation in contemporary society and the evolution of state operations and orientations.[5] While a great deal of effort has been exerted in fleshing out racial gaps in policy attitudes (Kinder and Sanders 1996; Kinder and Mendelberg 2000) and negative attitudes toward blacks more broadly (Sidanius et al. 2000), little research has sought to better understand the structural and organizational constraints that hinder marginalized groups as they, via their representatives, attempt to enter the mainstream and renounce their status in the category of "other." The multiracial coalitions currently being built and strengthened in Congress indicate an opportunity for representatives of these groups to create and sustain substantive institutional change that can reduce the cumulative effects of racial ordering and privilege in the legislative process, and provide a template for change in other branches and at other levels of government.

DISTRICT STATUS, MEMBER STATUS, AND MARGINALIZATION

> You feel the discrimination. You feel like you are being underestimated and undervalued. There's a constant struggle to be heard and you have to fight the undervaluing and the underestimation. What's worse, because you represent a certain constituency, your opinion doesn't carry weight.
>
> —Member 14, Latino, Southwest

The logic behind the argument that the demographic makeup of one's district or the racial background of a member of Congress can limit the ability of that member to represent their constituents may seem unclear. I argue that interpersonal dynamics in the House (including implicit negative racial stereotypes), concentrated marginalization in geographic districts, and the structural and organizational constraints inherent in the party system impact the legislative process in myriad ways. Negative stereotypes regarding racial minority groups often lessen the credibility of representatives from those groups, as well as the consequent ability they have to persuade their colleagues to provide support for legislative initiatives. Districts highly populated with people who lack societal status—in this case high concentrations of impoverished racial minorities—are more likely to have needs overlooked due to the interaction effects of both racism and class prejudice. Finally, the structural and organizational constraints that accompany the distribution of party resources (decisions usually made by leadership) also factor into the status of members from and representing marginal communities, and privilege certain members and districts over others in the policy process.

In effect, I argue that marginalization occurs within the House of Representatives as an entity unto itself, where both members *and* districts can be marginalized along multiple dimensions, although here I focus on a racial divide.[6] Two areas of literature might better explain the logic behind these arguments: the field of organizational behavior and psychology, and the theory of intersectionality. While the first topic focuses on intergroup relationships, the second addresses the complex dynamic of having multiple, overlapping forms of marginal status in play. Applied to congressional behavior, the organizational behavior literature can identify ways that the presence of diversity in the House of Representatives may result in subtle forms of racism that inhibit the legislative success of elected officials from and representing racial minority communities. Meanwhile, literature on intersectionality helps us approach the status of districts that experience the advanced marginalization of having large concentrations of *both* racial minorities *and* impoverished households.[7]

All too often, political institutions are portrayed as objective entities, independent in their ability to promote fairness and equality. Congress, like its counterparts, is not immune to the insidious nature of prejudice. These institutions were not built with the express intent to provide for the equal representation of racial minorities, women, the poor, or other groups that have suffered systematic exclusion from their ranks. That exclusion, and consequent discrimination, remain deeply entrenched in contemporary American society. Moreover, both negative and positive implicit associations are triggered by various descriptive cues such as race and gender. These associations occur during the development of public policy, offering many implications for the direction of the nation.

The exploration of the impact of racial order is not new to the study of American political development, though further research could and should be devoted to it. In *Civic Ideals*, Smith notes the prominence of group dominance during the formation of civic identity in American citizenship (1997). Specifically, he notes the ascriptive nature in defining Americanism, which has arisen out of inegalitarian racial, patriarchal, and religious terms (1997, 3). This prevalence has been variegated in manifestation, but often surfaced as a result of deep-rooted beliefs of inequality, commonly held by dominant groups. He argues that those in power have created citizenship laws that bolster the notion that control of the country rightfully belongs to wealthy, white, male, Protestant Anglo-Saxons (1997, 2–3). Thus, "many Americans have been attracted to ascriptive civic myths assuring them that, regardless of their personal achievements or economic status, their inborn characteristics make them part of a special community ... distinctively and permanently worthy" (38).

Indeed, racial orders prioritizing whites over non-whites have been predominant throughout US history (King and Smith 2005). Analyses of American political development have often omitted the prominence of race, despite considerable evidence suggesting a continuity of racialized policies (and race-exclusionary policies) crafted and overseen by persons disproportionately wealthy, white, and male. King and Smith advocate the use of a "racial institutional orders" approach to historical study precisely because it "helps explain many features of American politics that may appear *unrelated* to race, such as congressional organization, bureaucratic autonomy and modern immigration policies" (78).

To draw the connection to both member and district marginalization, we must consider the implication for leadership, governance, and policy prioritization. If many Americans accept these ascriptive myths that the United States rightfully belongs to wealthy, white, Anglo-Saxon, Protestant men, that dynamic may affect every level of the political process—from whether non-white men and women of all ethnicities receive electoral support, to successful passage of social justice programs disproportionately benefiting communities of color, women and children, religious minorities, and the poor.[8] Perhaps most pernicious is the likelihood that the arbiter or arbiters will already be wealthy, white, Anglo-Saxon, Protestant men. Even though poor persons, women, persons of color, and religious minorities can now be elected to Congress, whether they are viewed as equals within the body of government (as well as outside of it) is not automatic. Resource deprivation based upon social group statuses such as race, gender, class, and religion remains ever-present, in accordance with historic ascriptive myths of who is truly American.

Intergroup Dynamics and Racism in Context

Racial prejudice, and consequent discrimination, occurs through various methods and in differing circumstances in a wide range of environments, including congressional politics. Psychological research offers more information on implicit or subtle racism, which is further explored in research on group dynamics in organizations. Scholars have detailed not only the negative and positive implicit associations attached to race, gender, and age (Banaji and Bhaskar 2000; Dasgupta et al. 2000; Banaji 2001), but also the consequent discrimination that occurs in everyday situations, often as a result of those negative and positive associations (Ayres 1991, 2001). Discriminatory behavior and racial prejudice are not necessarily the results of animus; rather, they can also be the outcome of deeply entrenched stereotypes that unconsciously affect both individual choice and action (Cacioppo and Berntson 2002). Disparate treatment in housing and employment, where conduct in leasing and hiring is race- or gender-dependent, is not assumed to imply racial or gender animus, but nevertheless leads to unfair effects, often at the expense of the marginalized group involved in the transaction. Similarly, studies have found mounting evidence for racial discrimination in purchasing cars, workplace promotions, motor vehicle stops by police, and even in the number of fouls called in the National Basketball Association (the NBA).[9]

Devos and Banaji (2005) have found that in investigating the extent to which various ethnic groups are associated with the category of "American," studies consistently reveal that Asian Americans and African Americans remain less associated with America than their white counterparts. Despite explicit notions of egalitarian values, Devos and Banaji found notable evidence that "to be American is implicitly synonymous with being White" (447). This dynamic occurred across ethnic boundaries, showing that both racial minorities and whites held this similar attitude, though to varying degrees.

More broadly, Banaji has found strong automatic preferences for ingroups and that those preferences develop quickly and easily. Though not universal, and not equally strong, these attitudes are very prevalent in contemporary American society.

> Group membership effects on automatic attitude (i.e., liking for one's own group) are moderated by the evaluative imprimatur of the larger culture—members of groups that are socially liked, (i.e., considered "good") show stronger liking for their group (e.g., White Americans, females) than those who are, by comparison, not (Black Americans, males). (2001, 9)

In studies of the workplace, there exists a perplexing debate concerning the value of diversity, versus the difficulties inherent in heterogeneous group functioning. Some argue that increased diversity in workplace situations leads to greater innovation and creativity, thus resulting in better ideas and improved performance (Cox, Lobel, and McLeod 1991). In contrast, however, multiple dysfunctional dynamics have been noted in the increasingly diverse workforce, including increased stereotyping, significant in-group/out-group effects, and heightened interpersonal conflict (Messick and Massie 1989). When organizations operate with higher levels of diversity, observed conflicts over assigned tasks frequently become personal, negative stereotypes are invoked, and exclusionary behavior occurs.

To offer further understanding, O'Reilly et al. argue that the status judgments of individuals, particularly along the lines of race, ethnicity, and gender, typically reflect societal status hierarchies, where greater status is generally assigned to white males than to women and people of color (1998). Furthermore, they argue, women and people of color are more likely to suffer from derogatory stereotypes, because they have lower status in American society (1998, 189).

Should we assume that these organizational issues transfer onto political institutions generally, and on the US Congress in particular? The theoretical framework devised by political development scholars Orren and Skowronek suggests we can and should. They define "institutions" as organizations that (a) have broad but discernible purposes, (b) establish norms and rules, (c) assign roles to participants, and (d) have boundaries marking those inside and outside the institutions (2004, 82–85). Though classifiable as organizations, these political institutions carry significant weight outside of their internal boundaries, in that their actions (such as laws written, and resources distributed) have an impact much more far-reaching than the organization itself.

How do we incorporate this information from the fields of psychology and organizational behavior into our understanding of congressional behavior? With evidence detailing implicit negative associations of African Americans and other minorities as well as implicit associations of "American" equaling whiteness, it seems probable that these associations are held by many members of Congress, albeit at an unconscious level. Though held to varying degrees, and certainly not universal, negative implicit associations about marginal groups almost necessarily impact the quality of policy deliberation and implementation. In turn, these dynamics affect the treatment of members from and representing marginal groups by the larger political community.[10] That is, while there may be little racial animus detected or present, black and Latino lawmakers remain burdened by negative stereotypes, and underestimated in both their capabilities and their legitimacy. Many of the black and Latino members that I interviewed suggested that their experiences in the House of Representatives reflected subtle racism and microaggressions in the form of condescending remarks, dismissive comments, and the seeming inability of their colleagues to acknowledge their presence.

INTERSECTIONALITY

From another theoretical perspective, Kimberle Crenshaw offers insight into the overlapping and inter-relational dynamics of oppression (1989, 1991). The theory of intersectionality holds that classical models of oppression and dominance, such as race, ethnicity, gender, sexuality, and class, are not independent of one another. To the contrary, these dynamics interact with one another, creating unique, individual experiences of oppression. That is, the intersection of racism and sexism would make the experience of a black woman suffering from discrimination based upon her race and sex entirely distinct from the experience of a black man or a white woman. Similarly, to be a poor minority (and thus to suffer from both class and racial discrimination) would produce a different experience of oppression than to be singularly poor, or a wealthier minority. In essence, the intersection of class and race would result in multiple oppressions experienced simultaneously in a society already stratified by markers of marginalization.

One can easily draw the line between intersectionality at an individual level and interacting effects of discrimination at a collective level. The geographic concentration of intersecting types of oppression, specifically class and race, can be an unfortunate consequence of residential segregation, and is often reflected in electoral districts. That is, with residential segregation manifesting along the lines of class and race in neighborhoods and localities across the country (Massey and Denton 1993), high percentages of district populations are likely to share similar class and racial backgrounds. Districts with higher status populations are more likely to be privileged in the political process similar to other sectors. Meanwhile, marginal communities with less status never acquire the resources necessary to gain sufficient influence in the legislative process. With large concentrations of constituents that have been historically excluded by dominant power structures, there exists a greater cumulative effect of oppression, which can manifest as a lack of wealth and assets, lack of access to exclusive networks, and little to no insider understanding of policy issues and history, all of which are magnified in the geographic district model of representation.[11]

To be clear, if implicit negative associations about women and minorities exist in Congress just as they exist in everyday life, then representatives from those groups and representing those groups face an additional burden of overcoming those stereotypes, not only for themselves but also for their constituents. If certain populations suffer from multiple forms of oppression and have lower societal status, these dynamics substantially affect their ability to influence the political agenda, as well as the willingness of legislators to act on their behalf.[12]

Structural and Organizational Dynamics

Marginalization within the House can also come from multiple overlapping forces, including minority party membership; an ideological position that places one at the end of a spectrum where Democratic leadership takes one for granted; and holding a safe seat that the Democratic leadership does not worry about losing. Thus, in addition to the presence of unconscious stereotypes and discrimination, there are continuing structural and organizational dynamics at play, including the more pragmatic reality of majority rule, median votes, and the politics of swing districts and states.

Party leadership support for representatives can vary for multiple reasons, including the perceived safety of the district they represent, as well as the member's reliability to vote with the party on key issues. For survival purposes alone, majority party leadership may continually focus on maintaining their power through stronger support for swing districts and swing district candidates, which in recent years have lower percentages of minorities. Similarly, members who are taken for granted as safe votes, rather than swing votes, are not courted as heavily by leadership with earmarks set aside for district-related programs. The swing votes, usually identified as undecided members whose issue preferences cannot be easily determined, can sometimes be swayed by sweetened deals that enable them to "bring home the bacon."

How does this structural dynamic affect the position of members from and representing marginal communities? Moreover, how does this affect the districts they represent? An economic understanding of democracy (i.e., Downs 1957) provides further support for the notion that districts with sizable marginal populations will be overlooked or neglected in the legislative process precisely because they or their representatives are in the margins and far from the median. The incentive to provide party resources and electoral support to members from safe seats and who are not ideologically located near the median of Congress is minimal. Meanwhile, the decision to maintain power through addressing the needs of both the representatives and the constituents of swing districts can have a sizable benefit.

In turn, however, a majority party that does not tend to the needs of the swing districts and/or its candidates from swing districts is unlikely to maintain its power, and consequently unable to offer any assistance to members from and representing marginal communities. With the high rate of partisan polarization in more recent years, maintaining a majority party position is essential to achieving policy objectives.

MINORITY LEGISLATIVE INFLUENCE

Now I return to the study of influence, especially for lawmakers from and representing marginal communities. The term "influence" will extend broadly throughout the rest of this chapter, with multiple types of influence defined and expanded. For purposes here, we can approach the broad term of "political influence" as follows: the ability to successfully accomplish one's legislative policy agenda by both getting the legislation to the floor for a vote, and gaining the requisite number of votes necessary for passage, as well as ensuring that policy objectives that conflict with one's agenda are not passed by the full chamber. This approach is not limited to the behavior of lawmakers, but can be applied to groups and individuals involved in the process at various levels. Central to this particular section is the role of moneyed interests, committee assignments, and committee leadership in the advancement of specific legislation and broad policy agendas.

The influence of moneyed interests in the legislative process remains a prominent factor in the fundraising ability of lawmakers, the successful passage of bills, and the consequent success rate of their authors. In exploring the vote-buying dynamic, Hall and Wayman (1990) found that the effects of group expenditures surface more frequently at the committee level than on the floor, and that the money is used both to mobilize support, as well as demobilize opposition. Arguing that PACs are rational actors, special interests increase the likelihood of success through strategically contributing to members whose committee assignments overlap with the path of the legislation. Whether it buys votes or changes minds, Hall and Wayman contend that money buys members' time and access to the resources under their control. That access to the lawmaker is crucial in mobilizing members or providing disincentive to participate, according to the preferences of the PAC.

Evidence also suggests that social group identification, particularly along cleavages of race and sex, has a substantive role in legislative politics. Members of Congress not only have varying interests that they seek to advance through legislation, but they have different degrees of intensity with which they chose to wield their influence, revealed through the amount of time and energy they invest in a given issue or piece of legislation (Hall 1996). In multiple instances, the unknown factor in a political equation is the amount of influence a member of Congress is willing to wield in favor of legislation, effectively compelling his or her colleagues to comply with his or her wishes. Regarding identifications such as race, ethnicity, and gender, Hall finds support for the theory that the intensity of participation and members' personal policy commitments are influenced by their personal background and racial group identification. With regards to the Job Training Partnership Act of 1982, he reports:

> Black representatives were disproportionately represented on the originating committee, and a black member happened to be the subcommittee chair (and thus floor manager); . . . In short, the minority group identification of the member was responsible for increasing her involvement in this area, independent of the otherwise important effects of constituency and institutional position. (207)

Though somewhat unsurprising, many sources of garnering influence in the legislative process, such as fundraising and committee and subcommittee assignments, are the same arenas where it is wielded, thus creating a revolving cycle of concentrated power. These incentives and the amount of control exercised by party leadership (including the power to grant special rules to allow a bill to reach the floor for vote), extend to committee and subcommittee assignments, where the ability to draft and continually shape legislation is most heavily concentrated.

The ability of a collective group to wield influence in the legislative process, particularly for racial minorities, is the central focus of this story. In the field of political science, where minority representation has been given substantive attention, influence at the legislative level has been explored. David Canon's *Race, Redistricting and Representation* (1999) suggests that influence in the legislative arena includes not just the ability to get elected, but the ability to both positively and negatively influence legislation. In his analysis of the ability of the Congressional Black Caucus (CBC) to influence policy outcomes, members are able to use negative power, delaying and eliminating legislation that is not in accordance with their stance, but also ensuring the ultimate passage of policies that they support. According to Canon, the CBC provided the margin of victory on nine of the sixteen "key votes" identified by *Congressional Quarterly* in the 103rd Congress.[13]

What Canon omits, however, is that the 103rd Congress was an especially notable anomaly, in that it convened following the legislative redistricting of 1992, which included the creation of more than twenty new majority-minority districts, both black and Latino. This change effectively meant that more black and Latino representatives served in Congress than ever before. Another circumstance that played a crucial role in the minority influence over the political process had to do with partisan politics. At the time, all but one of the black members in the House of Representatives were members of the Democratic Party, which held the majority and determined the rules, as well as the agenda. With 39 members in the 258-member Democratic Caucus, black members constituted more than 15 percent of the entire party membership in the House—a significant number by most standards. Though they had numbers, with almost half of the CBC as freshmen members of the Democratic Caucus, they had little influence in the agenda-setting process of the 103rd Congress. Finally, with the CBC membership usually located to the far left of the political spectrum in Congress, it is doubtful that theirs were swing votes and that they might have voted differently. That is, while they had a significant number of votes to constitute the margin of victory, this fact did not mean that their votes determined the outcome, in that their support may have been assumed as certain.

Regardless, the tide turned with the Republican takeover of 1994. While the black membership remained virtually the same, the size of the Democratic Caucus shrank to 204 members, with the Republicans accounting for 230 representatives in the House. Without majority party status, the CBC had very little influence over agenda-setting and floor rules. It held no powerful committee chairmanships where its members could put forth or block legislation.

The newly crafted majority-minority districts in 1992 did lead to greater representative policy influence for minority legislators in the 103rd Congress, but the influence was short-lived, as a result of the Republican takeover in 1994, and mitigated by the freshman status of so many of the recently elected minorities. Although the expansion in numbers increased the overall stature of the Congressional Black and Hispanic Caucuses, organizational hurdles limited their legislative influence, followed by the partisan shift in power that curtailed it almost entirely.

The 2006 elections produced notable changes to these circumstances. Having gained years of seniority, combined with the new Democratic Party leadership, members of the Congressional Black Caucus and the Congressional Hispanic Caucus (CHC) secured demonstrable power in numerous arenas. Of the eighteen committees that had subcommittees in the 110th Congress, three were chaired by members of the Black Caucus, while two were chaired by members of the Hispanic Caucus. In addition, both the Committee on House Administration and the Committee on Standards of Official Conduct were chaired by members of the CBC.[14] In subcommittee chairmanships, the number of CBC chairs totaled 18 out of 101 subcommittees. The number of CHC subcommittee chairmanships rose to thirteen.[15] In both caucuses, certain members successfully obtained party leadership positions.

LEGISLATIVE BEHAVIOR AND PARTY TIES

One commonly accepted theory of congressional behavior offers some insight into the driving forces behind legislative politics, and the compelling interests that factor into the decisions of elected officials. Much of the conventional wisdom in political science holds that legislators are motivated by multiple dynamics, the most prominent being a desire to increase their political influence through loyalty to their party (Cox and McCubbins 1993, 2005). For elected officials from and representing marginal groups, some of these theories may not be as explanatory of legislative behavior as they are for the majority of legislators, while other theories do not consider the uniqueness of the position they are in. Though all members of Congress have multiple goals, reelection and toeing the party line may be lesser concerns to members representing marginal groups, due either to structural circumstances or the imminent needs of their constituency.

In *Legislative Leviathan* (1993) and then again in *Setting the Agenda* (2005), Cox and McCubbins make the argument that majority party members are united in their desire to keep their party in power and benefit from the perks of majority party status. Moreover, they see political parties as procedural cartels, where individual members are motivated to express loyalty to the party as a means of gaining power and influence in the legislative process. Members are united by a need to keep value in their party label, as the reputation of the party invariably affects their own personal chances for reelection. In turn, party leaders make sure that members have incentives to cooperate and promote party interests, either through the attainment of leadership positions themselves, committee chair status, greater influence in agenda-setting, or the increased likelihood of bill passage.

While extremely useful in understanding legislative politics, this theory requires small adjustments and caveats to better account for the influence of marginal groups in the policy process. In various ways, it has not taken into account the dynamic of marginal group status, where one's identity may play a role as a precursor to partisan membership and consequent participation.

A motivating factor of legislative behavior rarely discussed in great detail is the immediate and crucial needs of the constituencies that members from and representing racial minority groups serve. In disadvantaged communities with extensive poverty and few resources available to support families and provide for increased development, holding office provides the means to an end for a legislator as she tries to provide for constituent needs. Congress members from these districts may be much more concerned with their ability to help funnel jobs, healthcare, and educational opportunities to their constituents. Granted, meeting party goals remains a necessary component of this equation, but it is often less emphasized, given the urgent need to address the adverse conditions of those who elected the member.[16]

Cox and McCubbins's partisan rationale has many merits. Given the nature of the two-party system, legislators have tremendous incentive to follow leadership and toe the party line as a means of gradually gaining status within their party, and consequently having greater influence in setting the policy agenda. Their model, however, does not consider the position of representatives with marginal status, derived either from their personal or district attributes. The degree to which a legislator toes the party line may depend heavily on whether either party has actively taken up a broad civil rights agenda as a top priority. When members of Congress from and representing marginal groups advocate for the particular needs of the communities they represent, the party may choose to ignore their requests or even ostracize them as a result of their advocacy. This dynamic does not contrast with Cox and McCubbins's account of legislative politics, but it can further our understanding of legislators operating on behalf of those at the margins of society. Toeing the party line is more likely to directly conflict with the particular needs of marginal groups, and there is significant variation between the two prominent parties in American politics, especially in terms of their willingness to acknowledge marginalized communities and their unique needs.

Existing theories of Congress tend to assume that if one or two specific attributes of elected officials are known—their ideological location and their party—that is enough information to accurately characterize most of their behavior. Most analyses of Congress proceed from this vantage point, rendering the race or racial demographics of one's constituency, along with any other number of factors, obsolete. To a certain extent, this approach creates fairly accurate predictive models of legislative behavior. The trouble, however, remains the lack of nuance that arrives from better understanding how individual experiences, events, and histories shape ideology, and how ideology cannot be best demonstrated on a linear plane. Moreover, it is not simply that certain issues may be higher priorities for lawmakers from and representing marginalized communities; rather, it is that their willingness to provide strong support potentially increases their effectiveness in representation. In sum, by factoring in member and district attributes that might otherwise go unnoticed by most scholarship on legislative behavior, we add value to the equation.

At various points in American history, only one major party has advocated for racial minorities, and in many instances, no support has been offered from either party. In a situation where party leadership displays little interest in addressing issues that are particular to marginalized communities such as racial minorities, their representatives are in an unenviable position, forced to decide between two parties that opt not to prioritize their needs and interests. In contemporary US politics, the Democratic Party has displayed much greater interest in the circumstances of marginal groups. As of the 114th Congress, all but one floor-voting House member of the Congressional Black, Hispanic and Asian Pacific American (Executive Board) Caucuses were Democrats, out of seventy-six total. In addition, roughly 75 percent of the House floor-voting members of the Congressional Caucus for Women's Issues were Democrats (sixty-three out of eighty-five total). All six House members participating in the LGBT Equality Caucus were Democrats.

The question has arisen whether, in a realistic examination of party politics, the system allows for inclusive democracy (Frymer 1999). The very nature of parties, as they try to gain majority status or win the presidency, does not necessitate the embrace of a civil rights agenda. Frymer wrote:

> Scholars argue that competition between two parties forces at least one party to reach out to those groups not represented by the other party. As a result of this competition, parties will mobilize these groups to policy issues; educate and persuade other party members to support the interests of these marginalized groups; and finally, place the interest of these groups on the political agenda and represent them in the legislative arena. (6)

Using historical evidence, Frymer goes on to argue that parties actually have politically compelling reasons not to behave in this manner—and in fact, party leaders often resist mobilizing and incorporating blacks into the political system.

> The fear of the disruptive costs of advancing the cause of African-Americans precludes party leaders from prominently competing for the African-American vote. (46)

The consequent distancing of parties from blacks in particular and civil rights more broadly is seldom lost on legislators from and representing racially marginalized groups. For example, each year the Congressional Black Caucus submits its own recommended federal budget plan, arguing that their plan better addresses the needs of poor and disadvantaged communities across the country. The CBC puts forward this budget separately from either party, and without any party endorsement.

With regard to the marginal status of members on Capitol Hill, multiple circumstances must take place in order for members representing marginal groups to have influence: 1) those members must be in the majority party that controls the legislation that is passed by the committee; 2) they must have enough seniority to gain chair status; and 3) party leadership must be willing to advocate for marginal group interests, or at least not opt to circumvent the committee process, as seen in recent years. Until 2007, all three of these conditions were not met, rendering those from and representing marginal groups with limited political leverage, and consequent influence over the policies that were both passed out of committee and considered on the House floor. Legislation and amendments proposed by those representing racial minorities and categorized as "civil rights" were repeatedly defeated by the Republican Party, and the information that those members offered seemed to be of little consequence in the legislative process.

Members from and representing racial minority groups do have a very high stake in being in the majority party, especially given the heightened polarization in Congress, combined with GOP hostility toward issues linked to blacks, Latinos, and other marginalized communities. Though their safe seats may mean they derive less benefit from the party reputation, per Cox and McCubbins (1993), majority status means chairmanships, better committee assignments, and the ability to offer input into the policy agenda. The tension that arises in this partisan issue stems from the fact that white Democrats may seek majority party status by moderating the party image, and thus distancing themselves from traditional liberal ideas that have appeal in black and Latino communities. In effect, a "good" party reputation that can win white suburbs or swing districts may mean legislative and campaign behavior that is inimical to the interests and preferences of members from and representing racial minorities.

While the partisan theory of legislative behavior leads to logical conclusions, the relative position of representatives from and representing marginal groups has been notably overlooked. In recent years, with Republican control of both the House and the Senate, and increasingly strong party leadership, the committee process (where there is greatest ability to amend legislation) in the House has been rendered virtually inconsequential in the actions of the whole congressional body. The conservative nature of House leadership since 1994 has resulted in limited gains for members from and representing racially marginal groups, who tend to support more liberal policies that protect marginalized communities. As a consequence, the interests of marginal groups such as racial minorities, women and children, the LGBT community, and the poor have been at best ignored, and at worst, actively opposed.

GROUP STATUS, LINKED FATE, AND COALITION-BUILDING IN THE HOUSE OF REPRESENTATIVES

At this point, we have sufficient reason to believe that marginalization occurs in the legislative process, and that congressional research often overlooks the role of race and the racial demographics of districts as factors in legislative behavior. How do representatives respond to the marginalization that occurs in the process? I argue that those from and representing marginal groups, bolstered by increased numbers in the early 1990s, and in response to extreme marginalization that occurred during the Republican control of the House from 1994 to 2006, built and maintained coalitions to gain political influence in the process. Those alliances were forged, in large part, as the result of feelings of linked political fate, shared to particularly high degrees by those advocating for racial minorities. While these coalitions were built in response to

Republican marginalization, they now provide the foundation for a powerful voting bloc within the Democratic Party.

In this section, I explain and expand my theory of linked political fate, which I believe is critical to understanding the representation of marginal groups, especially for racial minorities. Lawmakers from and representing racial minorities often bear the heavy burden of improving conditions in their communities, and so they must be strategic in their attempts to meet the needs of their constituents. There is a decided utility in building alliances in Congress, but for racial groups and others suffering from advanced marginalization, it is a dire necessity. In many cases, they believe that the political fate of the particular group or groups that they are advocating for is inextricably linked to the fate of another marginal group. This dynamic, in and of itself, can account for many instances of legislative behavior that could mistakenly be interpreted as partisan attachment. For instance, when black, Latino, and Asian Pacific American members of the House of Representatives vote together with other members of their party caucus, it could be mistakenly attributed to a need to toe the party line. In reality, however, depending upon the policy issue, their motivation may have more to do with a cross-racial alliance than it does with the prioritization of partisan affiliation. Moreover, their ideological points may be inaccurately assessed, as this dynamic goes unaccounted for in most congressional scholarship.

The use of coalitions as a means to broaden and increase political strength is by no means new to the political process. But the fact that members of Congress from and representing marginal groups would choose to embrace this tactic as a means for survival and advocacy invites new understanding of how and when these coalitions are built. In order to have sufficient influence to achieve a solid voice in the deliberative process of US legislative bodies, alliances are repeatedly forged among representatives that may seem to conflict when considering the preferences of their constituencies, producing a "Grass Roots vs. Grass Tops" effect. Having historically been shut out of traditional avenues of influence, legislators from and representing marginal groups are compelled to participate in coalitional politics, building bonds with other marginal groups as a means to increase their numbers and successfully pass legislation.

The power of intergroup coalitions throughout legislative history is well documented. In *Disjointed Pluralism*, Eric Schickler argues that coalitions have driven the regimes of institutional change in the United States (2001). The pluralism that Schickler refers to is the vast quantity of collective interests that cooperate with each other at certain moments and compete against each other in other instances over power within legislative politics, in many cases spurring innovative change. Examining four specific periods of institutional change, it is evident that policy interests (not necessarily partisan interest) have done much to challenge and shape the direction of the national legislature.

Legislative coalition-building should not be seen as merely the bond between separate, mutually exclusive groups. In many cases, it must be seen as the manifestation of overlapping identities and the increased understanding of, and support for, "cross-cutting issues," that is, issues that disproportionately and directly affect only one segment of one or many marginal groups (Cohen 1999). The increased attention to cross-cutting issues provides a foundation for multiracial coalitions in representation. For example, domestic violence is sometimes viewed as a women's and children's issue, yet it has a drastic impact across racial boundaries. While child abuse and spousal abuse do not universally impact communities of color, they nonetheless are growing concerns that have been increasingly adopted by indigenous organizations specifically geared toward representing the interests and preferences of African American and Latino communities.[17] Thus, these issues can be unifying across racial lines, not simply within them.

According to Cohen, cross-cutting issues often engage more than one primary identity, including but not limited to race, gender, sexuality, and class (1999). While consensus issues—issues that are viewed as universal to society, or at least to a particular subgroup—have been consistently owned by those various communities and subgroups, they are not the only policies that should be addressed and remedied. Awareness of various cross-cutting issues such as domestic violence, mental health, and

HIV/AIDS prevention have led to a shift in issue advocacy, where these issues are increasingly seen as concerns fundamental to particular groups and to a larger society as a whole.

Within marginalized groups, particularly the African American community, Michael Dawson has argued that there exists a linked fate—the belief that one's life chances are inextricably tied to the racial group one belongs to—perceived and understood by blacks, and that this understanding of linked fate motivates and even mobilizes black voters (1994). Given a history of oppression, where race has been a decisive factor in determining the life chances of African Americans regardless of whatever economic status achieved, voting behavior was motivated along the lines of perceived racial group interest. Perceptions of self-interest are explicitly linked to perceptions of racial group interests, leading voters to use a shortcut—namely, a black utility heuristic—to make political decisions.[18]

Should we explore this idea at a more macro-level understanding of the political process, it becomes clear that there is a decided utility in building alliances between and among marginal groups as a means to amass critical numbers in the majority rule system. For some members, there is little choice in the matter. Without allies with whom one shares common goals, legislative success will never occur. In order to reach the 218 votes in the House of Representatives, or the 51 votes in the Senate, legislators from and representing marginal communities must reach out to others as a means to advocate the interests of their districts. This is not simply a manifestation of practical politics. Among marginal groups, the overarching consensus issues tend to be equality, fundamental fairness, and social justice.

The decision to coalesce among representatives of communities of common interest may lead to unwanted consequences. That common interest can become tenuous when voters disagree with the foundation of a political platform espoused. In these instances, trade-offs are made in order to best serve the interests of one's constituent base. While building and maintaining these alliances, a member may go against her own personal preferences in order to better advocate for the district represented. She may also build alliances that voters dislike. At times, coalitional politics can be more of a compromise than a trade, in that it may be the manifestation of a member's personal ideological agenda, rather than a calculus used to achieve power.

Take, for example, the devoutly religious wing of the black community. Believing that homosexuality is a sin, high levels of anti-gay sentiment and intolerance have been continually demonstrated in this group, with a large percentage of black churches condemning the gay rights movement, particularly gay marriage. Nevertheless, most of the black members of Congress (who largely represent this wing) have repeatedly opted to oppose the conservative gay marriage ban brought forth by the Republican Party and supported by their constituents.

What happens when the personal ideologies and political calculus of elites, particularly legislators, are not in accord with their constituent opinions? In coalition-building among marginal groups, a legislator may overlook the *preferences* of his or her constituents as a means to better serve their *needs* and *interests*, so long as those particular preferences are not as salient as other issues supported by the representative. This dynamic, of course, is contextual, and not specific to marginal group representation. Issues such as immigration and gay marriage may be salient in some districts, though not particularly salient in others. Significant variation exists in attitudes within marginalized communities, depending upon factors such as geographic location, level of participation in various community institutions, and ability to trust in and unite behind the leadership of political elites. Regardless, legislators representing marginal groups may choose to privilege needs over preferences in the political process. The immediate needs of housing, healthcare, and education often trump preferences such as banning gay marriage or building a fence across the US-Mexico border.

For example, a member of the Congressional Black Caucus may choose to vote against the preferences of his or her constituents on an issue such as immigration. Even if support for the measure is high and salient in the district, she may see this as a preference of her constituency, but nevertheless deem this preference as less important than a need, or even counter to the best interests of her constituency. If and when legislation is deemed unnecessary for the district, discriminatory in nature, or counter to political alliances already in place, principles of anti-discrimination and coalitional politics become more prominent factors than constituent preferences in determining legislative behavior, particularly for members from and representing marginal groups.

The majority rule system in legislative politics, combined with the relatively small number of members from and representing marginal groups, affects their ability to influence policy. I argue that a *linked political fate* is shared by multiple marginalized groups (including but not limited to racial minorities, women and children, and the LGBT communities) that have immediate, unaddressed needs; this fate is often understood by legislators though it may or may not be recognized at the constituency level. That is, the political fates of various marginalized groups are directly linked to the fates of other marginalized groups. Marginal group status affects the political chances of legislation benefiting constituencies in need. Members from and representing these districts have an acute awareness of this linked fate in the political realm, and most act accordingly through coalition work, issue advocacy, and voting behavior.

To be clear, this linked political fate is not essentially partisan, despite the partisan distribution of those representing marginalized communities. The fate is linked by political and social attitudes toward difference and the policies one supports, or even formulates, on the basis of that predisposition toward difference. Groups that have been systematically categorized as the "other" and consequently denied access to dominant structures of government share a linked political fate. Though their histories may be varied, most of their representatives recognize that they cannot afford to support efforts to legitimize discriminatory practices, as that legitimacy may return to haunt them.[19] That is, discrimination that is justified against one marginal group provides the means to justify discriminatory practices toward other groups. In turn, the unfortunate social circumstances of marginal groups intensify the willingness of lawmakers advocating for those groups to adhere to principle, as well as a desire to increase the odds in their favor through classical political calculus.

In some cases, members representing these groups may be unified through principles such as anti-discrimination, anti-poverty, or anti-violence. These principle-based coalitions among legislators, like cross-cutting issues, build the foundation for multiracial cooperation in the House of Representatives. Members unite around progressively principled solutions to healthcare, welfare, crime, and education. They can also unite around the need for their constituents to benefit from equal opportunity and access to the dominant social, political, and economic structures.

In other cases, members may choose to unite based not upon principle, but upon political calculus and a more general understanding that offering support for certain policies that do not affect a large portion of their constituencies may still yield future support for concerns more closely linked in their constituencies. For instance, while issues such as gay marriage and immigration may be perceived to have limited direct impact on African Americans, most members of the Congressional Black Caucus have offered support for liberal immigration policies and have denounced proposed constitutional amendments to ban gay marriage. Some members do this not because of principles of anti-discrimination, but because they seek support for their issues in return.[20]

Linked political fate differs significantly from common interest among groups, in part as a result of continued exclusion and marginal status. To be sure, many lawmakers from and representing marginal groups have common interests and cultivate opportunities for mutually beneficial alliances. Linked political fate, however, comes from an understanding that these alliances are not only beneficial—they are, in fact, crucial to the political strength, and even to the survival, of the group. It represents a belief that should one group be sacrificed or blamed for societal maladies, another group with marginal status may be the next culprit in line for derision.

The language of civil rights and those groups included under its banner have broadened over time. At one point, the inclusion of women, Latinos, and the LGBT community under the umbrella of civil rights would have been unheard of and largely rejected by African American organizations.

As times have changed, organizations such as the Leadership Conference for Civil Rights have adopted new measures for inclusion that more ably encompass groups other than African Americans that have suffered systemic marginalization. A common theme, reflecting a negligence on behalf of mainstream society to acknowledge the prevalent needs and interests of these marginal groups, has resulted.

As organizations have changed and adapted, so too has the representation of marginal groups, particularly racial minorities. The chairs of the Congressional Black, Hispanic, and Asian Pacific American Caucuses meet regularly to discuss upcoming issues and policies. In so doing, they better ensure that members of the Congressional Tri-Caucus gain important information concerning policy stances, and in turn that those policy stances will be voiced during various phases of deliberation. In addition, the leadership encourages the entire membership of the three caucuses to attend annual retreats and health summits, where they can update each other on the needs and interests of their communities, building bridges in an effort to ensure future legislative success.

CONSTITUENT POLICY INFLUENCE

While the caucuses have adapted to the changing times and the increasing need for inter-group coalitions that add considerable breadth to their strategies to gain influence, it seems the courts have maintained narrow measurement standards for influence, combined with vague arguments regarding their role in the legislative redistricting process. Recent court definitions have been insufficient in exploring and defining influence for minority communities and other marginal groups. The primary definitions of influence have focused almost solely upon electoral influence, where the ability to influence an election using voter participation in a local arena is an adequate measure of minority political power. Relying heavily on percentage voting age populations as indicators of influence on overall policy outcomes, courts spend little energy exploring the circumstances under which influence can actually be exercised, necessitating a remedy that is more informed by context (the likes of which Cohen advanced in her three main principles, outlined in the first chapter).

A more pertinent question is how this type of district might affect a representative's voting behavior and representation style—that is, how much a representative's constituents might effectively influence his or her policy decisions. In studying legislative behavior, there are variations in approach to representation. Some elected officials see themselves as trustees, elected with a sufficient level of autonomy to deliberate and act in favor of the greater common good and national interests, even if it means going against the short-term interests of their constituencies. Others see themselves as delegates, reflecting the preferences of their constituents with little individual autonomy.[21] Regardless of their race, representatives of influence districts may not be able to best represent their African American constituents if they feel equally constricted by their conservative white voters. Should one represent a district with high levels of racial polarization, combined with roughly equal levels of black Democrats and white Republicans, a representative is faced with a difficult balancing act. In this case, to maintain her seat, her better judgment may be mitigated by a desire for reelection. A desire to participate in certain coalitions would be effectively stifled by unknown or volatile electoral situations.[22]

In constituent policy influence, responsiveness to the needs of constituents takes the highest priority. Again, we return to a definition of political influence as the ability to accomplish a legislative agenda, and also prevent conflicting legislation from being passed through both houses and signed into law. To do this, constituent and interest groups advocating for racially marginalized communities often need advanced forms of mobilization, access to financial capital and issue expertise, and capable leadership able to persuade elected officials unfamiliar with specific issues to vote in their favor.

How do marginal groups, who have already been excluded from dominant forms of political influence, convince legislators without sizable marginal populations to act on their behalf? Perhaps the most prominent issue with constituent policy influence is not whether constituents influence the decisions of their representatives. Most representatives would argue that they do, and that they are far more willing to grant access and personal time to their constituents from back home. The issue remains that marginal groups do not have sizable constituencies in a majority of districts across the country. In fact, 308 congressional districts (roughly 71 percent of the nationwide total) have white supermajorities comprising more than 70 percent of the voting age population. In most districts, the proportion of racial minorities is even lower, often below 20 percent. While specific strategies such as getting in early and maintaining a presence (to be discussed later in this section) may increase their odds, it may not be enough to make them favorable.

Compelling an elected official to behave in accordance with constituent or group interests requires information that she may or may not have. It also requires an ability to convey a need that she may not be able to relate to on a personal level. Increased levels of responsiveness seem logical when the individual or group is seen as much more crucial to the survival of a politician, through the ability to deliver votes or campaign donations that are likely to result in greater name recognition and more votes. For marginal groups, who by sheer numbers do not have sizable populations in most districts, the ability to convince some members to vote favorably can be a monumental task.

Mayhew's theory of reelection in the case of constituent policy influence is important here. When constituent support for an issue is strong, both in terms of a sizable majority in favor of it, as well as a high level of issue salience, an elected official has a level of comfort in assuming that a strong stance will not compromise his or her job. Some contemporary civil rights issues are highly polarizing, with firm stances held on both sides—the most readily apparent being gay rights, particularly gay marriage, and immigration issues involving Latinos. To the extent that one side is more popular than another, it can be exceedingly difficult to ask an elected official to risk reelection, no matter how deserving the principle. Thus, the degree to which a legislator can be influenced by interest groups, be they marginal or otherwise, is still subject to the perceived electoral restraints of that legislator.

For marginalized groups, a unique position in society requires even more involved strategies to influence and change societal policies in a manner that better reflect their needs. In many instances, legislators without large marginalized communities in their districts remain unaware of the preferences of marginal groups, in that they may lack the shared experiences and understanding necessary to obtain similar perspective. In order to gain leverage in the legislative process, marginal groups need to "get in early"—and by this I mean maintaining a strong presence beginning early on in the policy formulation process—a key tactic to increasing the odds of favorable outcomes. By "getting in early," I include preemptive actions, where organizations establish rapports with various members and express their policy stances well before a bill reaches the committee process, and if possible, before an issue is even drafted into bill form. "Maintaining a strong presence" refers more to a general practice within the process. Organizations advocating for various issues and against others need to keep themselves on the radar of elected officials, so that they and their issues are not forgotten.

Getting in early is imperative to legislative success. On any number of bills, organizations advocating for marginal community interests will find that elected officials have already committed to favor the opposition, without realizing that a specific piece of legislation will have an adverse effect on communities of color, for example. This commitment is not necessarily made with malicious intent, but nevertheless it has a detrimental effect on racial minorities. To prevent this, groups advocating for marginal communities must approach the legislative process in a preemptive fashion, and endeavor to build relationships with all members, including those some might consider adversaries.

Maintaining a strong presence throughout the legislative process is a costly and daunting task, particularly for disadvantaged groups. This presence often includes attendance at fundraisers, town hall meetings, policy issue hearings, and other events, in addition to scheduling time with individual legislators both in the district and in Washington. Groups advocating on behalf of marginal communities must have the necessary staff, funds, and training to be successful in this area. Funding is primary, in part because staff retention and more general resource distribution are integral to the advocacy process. Turnover can come at the cost of continued successful relationships with legislators. Complicating the situation is the degree to which advocates will commit to marginal group interests. Strolovitch has found that non-governmental organizations who advocate for marginal groups seldom fully commit to the endeavors.

> Organizations are substantially less active when it comes to issues affecting disadvantaged subgroups than they are when it comes to issues affecting more advantaged subgroups. In spite of sincere desires to represent disadvantaged members, organizations downplay the impact of such issues and frame them as narrow and particularistic in their effect, while framing issues affecting advantaged subgroups as if they affect a majority of their members and have a broad and generalized impact. (Strolovitch 2006, 894)

Both of these strategies (getting in early and maintaining a strong presence) are difficult for varied reasons. To act preemptively, one must have access to information that is seldom published or available to the public. That is, advocates for marginal groups must be able to persuade legislators to behave favorably before members publicly commit to supporting a specific position. Similarly, maintaining a presence requires significant human capital well-versed in the political process. Marginal groups, especially those suffering from higher levels of economic depression, may not be able to meet the logistical hurdles necessary to get in early or maintain an active presence from start to finish. Unable to secure the human and financial capital for legislative success, these communities face unfavorable odds.

One manifestation of a lack of constituent policy influence can be identified not only in the passage of legislation already identified by individuals or groups as adversely affecting marginal groups or specifically benefiting the advantaged subgroups of society; it can also be found in last-minute changes to legislation occurring almost immediately preceding a floor vote. Policies that provide indirect benefits to racial minority groups may not be valued to the same degree as those that do not. For example, bipartisan legislation, the Safe Port Act of 2006 agreed to in conference with the Senate, initially included provisions to protect metropolitan transit in urban areas—services that are disproportionately used by racial minorities. When the conference report made it to the floor, the urban transit provisions were no longer in the text of the bill, unbeknownst to the minority party.[23] The opportunity to provide aid to a service disproportionately serving minorities and those without their own form of personal transportation was dropped, and deemed by the committee chair to be less important than other provisions of the bill. Said Representative Thompson of Mississippi:

> But despite all our efforts, at the end of the day this measure falls short. Once again House Republicans have turned their back on everyday working folks who rely on buses and trains to get to work. When offered an opportunity by the Senate to secure our mass transit and rail security they chose to do nothing . . . H.R. 4954, as passed by the House, was a good bill overall. The Senate improved upon the bill by, among other things, addressing rail and mass transit security. Unfortunately, this sham conference process denied consideration of the Senate ideas as well as Democratic amendments to better protect our Nation. And that, after this body overwhelmingly approved my motion to instruct the conferees to accept the Senate position on rail and mass transit security, the conference Chair denied the will of this body.[24]

Another caveat to constituent policy influence that impacts the representation of an elected official is his or her desire to gain statewide office.[25] Should a member of the House of Representatives be considering a future run for a statewide office, he or she may already be calculating a position that is palatable to an entire state, rather than a smaller, more immediate district. The median voter of an entire state is seldom located at the same ideological point as the median voter of a district, especially when the district has higher concentrations of racial minorities and impoverished communities than the state itself. As a result, members of the House representing sizable populations of marginal groups, but simultaneously angling for statewide positions in the future, may opt for more conservative platforms as a means to cater to a more conservative median voter.

So the question remains, how can a racial minority group convince legislators without sizable minority populations to act on its behalf? Though some strategies increase the odds for success, they may not be enough to make them favorable. Instead, the minority group may become heavily reliant on "surrogate representatives" from other geographic areas willing to champion their interests in the legislative process.

REPRESENTATIVE POLICY INFLUENCE

How effective are representatives at influencing policy outcomes? How much influence do they wield in the legislative process? Legislators from and representing racial minorities have often been shut out of traditional avenues of influence due to their marginal status or that of their district. Given that political capital is not evenly distributed in Congress, representatives from disadvantaged groups may have a significantly more difficult experience in wielding power among their colleagues. Consequently, legislators with marginal status have adopted progressive coalition-building as the most successful means to providing for their constituents, offering both direct and indirect benefits.

For elected officials, the ability to garner and wield influence in the legislative process requires the ability to effectively influence policy outcomes. In most cases, they are persuading other legislators to join with them on a vote, cosponsor a bill, or provide other means of public and private support for policy initiatives. A myriad of interacting circumstances and conditions including party control, common cause, political calculation, interpersonal dynamics, issue expertise, fundraising ability, committee assignments, and seniority all contribute to an individual legislator's ability to compel his or her colleagues into alignment.

Traditional avenues of influence, such as seniority, fundraising, and committee assignments, all weigh heavily in the policy process. The ability to get elected, access political donors, and gain exclusive committee as-signments motivates members of Congress to win reelection, and to raise money for their own campaign funds, as well as party dues. The nature of fundraising as a means to pay party dues, and thus improve one's internal status in the party, is of particular consequence for legislators from and representing marginal communities. If one represents a district where a majority of the support base is impoverished, raising money puts a legis-lator in the position of having to pander to well-funded special interests outside of their community in order to maintain high status in the eyes of party leadership, who then decides committee assignments.

Another aspect for consideration is the ability to gain office in the House of Representatives, and how common stepping stones to Congress disproportionately benefit those with greater resources. Many members of Congress served in state legislatures prior to serving in the House or Senate. Most of those state legislatures do not meet year round and offer only part-time salaries for elected officials. These positions allow little by way of flexible schedules, whereby a state legislator could maintain a second job to make ends meet, and even when not in session, these leg-islators have leadership responsibilities to the constituencies that hired them. Here, the implications for marginal communities and disadvan-taged subgroups of society are vast. Unable to afford to take months from their work schedules to participate in state government as legislators, con-stituents from economically disadvantaged groups (regardless of race) are effectively deterred from running for office, due to the practical reality of paying their bills and potentially supporting a family. When policy is made, and deliberation takes place, it is almost guaranteed that the socio-economic diversity of voices needed for sound lawmaking will be absent.

In my interviews, members of Congress repeatedly told me that a pri-mary objective of building and sustaining the Congressional Tri-Caucus was to maintain an active "voice in the room" at all times. While orga-nization advocates might be able to voice their opinions in private meet-ings, the members themselves could take strong stances at all stages in the policy process—provided they had someone in the room. With seventy to eighty floor-voting members of the Tri-Caucus in any given session of the House of Representatives, and another five non-floor-voting members who still serve on committees and gain seniority, they now have enough voices to make sure their opinions are recognized in subcommittee mark-ups and hearings, committee markups and hearings, and in conference with the Senate. In short, although they cannot guarantee a favorable out-come, they can forcefully advocate for the priorities and needs of black, Latino, and Asian Pacific American communities nationwide.

Comprising roughly one-sixth of the House of Representatives offers additional tangible benefits, among them an increased likelihood that members of the Congressional Tri-Caucus would not be put in the po-sition of being the only racial minority in the room. The isolation once experienced by these members individually no longer exists as a result of the collective. In turn, members of the Tri-Caucus can provide each other with vocal support, thereby strengthening the power of claims made, and hopefully providing valuable input into policy formulation.

The ability to achieve party status and plum committee assignments, and even the ability to gain election to Congress, all present hurdles to marginal groups that have been historically excluded from the process. With the formation of the Tri-Caucus, however, members from and rep-resenting racial minority communities increase their influence through vocal advocacy at each and every stage of the legislative process. Their increased numbers, particularly in the committee process, translates to the reduced ease with which they might be willfully dismissed by their opposition. As such, although the hurdles these members face are de-monstrably greater than those of their white counterparts, the formation of the Tri-Caucus improves upon their avenues for advocacy.

MARGINALIZATION AND THE STATUS QUO

It is equally important not only to describe the adverse circumstances that marginal groups experience and bear the burden of, but also to shift the focus of analysis to those structures and processes that allow certain forms of inequality to perpetuate. In *Inclusion and Democracy* (2000),

Iris Marion Young makes the argument that difference, such as race and gender, is not a problem unto itself. Rather, she maintains, it is that democratic processes do not take existing structural differences (such as institutional procedures) into account. Inclusion of difference does not necessitate a focus upon those who have been excluded, but rather on the structures that privilege certain groups, social perspectives, and modes of expression above others.

Contemplating institutional change only emphasizes the lack of focus on overarching structural privilege. Eric Schickler (2001) provides a comprehensive analysis of congressional development in *Disjointed Pluralism: Institutional Innovation and the Development of the U.S. Congress* and discusses the nature of change within Congress. Based upon historical research, he argues that congressional development is "disjointed in that members incrementally add new institutional mechanisms without dismantling preexisting institutions and without rationalizing the structure as a whole" (17–18). In addition, reform attempts have been mired down by a marked tendency to cater to the status quo. Schickler argues that "the effectiveness of institutional change has repeatedly been compromised by the need to accommodate a preexisting authority structure that privileged other interests" (252).

Jost and Banaji (1994) go so far as to make the claim that humans consciously and unconsciously bolster the status quo in everyday situations. They advance a theory of system justification, defined as "the process by which existing social arrangements are legitimized, even at the expense of personal and group interest." Built off of group justification theories, where the dominance or hegemony of one group over another is rationalized, system justification stresses accommodation of the status quo, even by groups that have been systematically disadvantaged by that very status quo. That is, group hierarchy and social status is maintained not only through the in-group favoritism of the dominant, but also through the complacence and the out-group favoritism of the subordinate (Jost et al. 2004, 885).

If status quos and preexisting authorities remain privileged in the structural nature of legislative government, where does this leave groups that have been systematically excluded from the legislative process? When we shift the focus of analysis from the marginal experience to the structures that enable privilege to begin with, it seems that the system itself perpetuates the dominance of privileged elites. Periods of congressional reform, when institutional change has generally occurred, have been few and far between. The changes that have taken place over the last two centuries have still managed to accommodate or appease the dominant powers already in place. For groups that have been excluded from dominant structures and political institutions, to merely be present and accounted for in the democratic process does not mean that they will be afforded the necessary authority to effect change. With districts deplete of resources, and the lack of influence necessary to obtain resources for their districts, representatives from and representing marginal groups, politically speaking, are left with little leverage in the process. Their ability to gain access, however, to traditional avenues of political influence increases their leverage substantially.

CONCLUSION

The increasing attention to and ownership of cross-cutting issues by racial minority groups indicate growing influence and the lessening of marginalization for subgroups that exist as small segments within already marginalized communities. Rising concerns about issues formerly unaddressed in minority communities, such as HIV/AIDS, mental health, and domestic violence, all reflect changing dynamics in the internal politics of "civil rights" agenda-setting. In addition, the increasingly broad "civil rights" umbrella represents a greater willingness toward building coalitions that will advocate for marginal groups and in favor of policies that better address their substantive needs.

Although cross-cutting issues and marginal group coalitions have increased in visibility, they cannot be properly attended to if legislators from and representing marginalized communities lack influence at the representative levels of the democratic process. That is, even if constituents and advocacy groups are able to influence the opinions of their representatives, demonstrating the importance and urgency of both universal and cross-cutting issues, the likelihood of change may remain exceedingly low if those representatives lack the influence necessary to pass legislation aimed at improving the conditions of these groups with specialized needs.

That marginalized groups often lack access to traditional avenues of garnering influence furthers a cycle of marginalization. Their want of resources manifests through multiple structural processes. Without the competitive advantage needed to gain positions of power within the legislative body, representatives from and representing districts with high percentages of racial minorities will have little power to propose substantive changes in policy or to veto policies that adversely affect their constituents. In these situations, the needs of the groups that they represent will be disregarded. Similarly, marginal group status, which manifests both through the descriptive characteristics of members, as well as in the descriptive characteristics of the district they represent, can affect the perceived legitimacy of an elected official. In turn, this perceived lack of legitimacy may inhibit the ability to meet the needs of their constituents.

This chapter addresses issues of influence in the legislative process and the unique problems for marginal groups at multiple levels of the process. Constituents and their advocates who enter into the legislative fray in an effort to create change have specific obstacles to successful completion of their tasks. Not only must they enter into the debate earlier and at higher levels of organization, but in most cases they have limited resources of time, money and networks and connections that could better ensure their success.

Representatives from and representing minority communities are often subject to similar experiences, and are compelled to build coalitions as a result. They must rely on a different set of resources, such as seniority, fundraising and committee assignments (all of which seem to work in tandem) in order to gain greater influence in the policy process. Though lacking in numbers, those representing marginal groups, both from an advocacy group perspective and as elected officials, need alternative strategies and plans to not only prevent situations from worsening, but to actively improve upon the status quo.

As such, those representatives from and representing racial minority groups opt to build multiracial coalitions—particularly with representatives from other racially marginalized communities—so that their influence on policy outcomes is maximized, and the likelihood for success increases significantly. Based on a foundation of a perceived linked political fate, where the groups' prospects depend upon the strength gained from numbers, these burgeoning coalitions reflect greater changes we can expect in years to come.

Minority Voting Rights in Historical Context

It seems our fate never to get rid of the Negro question. No sooner have we abolished slavery than a party, which seems to be growing in power, proposes Negro suffrage, so that the problem—What shall we do with the Negro—seems as far from being settled as ever. In fact it is incapable of any solution that will satisfy both North and South.[1]

All too often, issues of legitimacy and inclusion rear their ugly heads in American politics. Who is allowed to participate in policymaking processes, and under what constraints, is a question that has been and remains highly contentious. The incremental, begrudging democratization of the American policy process has been rife with tension, both because certain groups were prioritized over others (often pitting them against one another) and because governments have actively sought to circumvent, if not outrightly dismiss, statutory and constitutional protections for those groups.

The foundation for minority influence in the contemporary policy process and the potential for progressive, interracial coalitions took root during the Reconstruction period, suffered throughout the nadir and Jim Crow, then reemerged in the period post-WWII, giving way to the most groundbreaking federal enforcement provisions in American history. The Civil Rights Act of 1964 and the Voting Rights Act (VRA) of 1965 targeted the most entrenched and overt forms of racial discrimination in the United States. Unparalleled in terms of legislative achievement, the former directly addressed racial discrimination in public accommodations, public schools, housing, employment, labor unions and economic opportunity, while the latter focused on the ability for persons of color to achieve representation in all levels and branches of government, and curtailed state- and municipal-level plans for minority exclusion. These successes could not have occurred without deliberate action by a liberal coalition of organizations, which in turn facilitated vast changes both in congressional makeup and legislative procedure. Included in this coalition were the civil rights community, New Deal liberals, academia, religious associations, and labor (Zelizer 2004). That all three branches of federal government were in accord on the issue of racial discrimination (albeit briefly) fostered an environment conducive to sweeping statutory change at the federal level.

Passage of the VRA in August 1965 marked a triumph for those who fought to secure the right to vote for people of color, and to end the strategies of minority exclusion that characterized many practices across the nation. With the possible exception of legislation enacted in 1957, enforcement of the Fifteenth Amendment was notably absent following the period of Reconstruction. Due in large part to the Compromise of 1877, when Republican presidential candidate Rutherford B. Hayes received Southern support in exchange for federal relaxation of Reconstruction efforts, the "negro question" was deemed a matter of regional concern, and thus government intervention came to an abrupt halt. Consequently, the political status of blacks fell off the national agenda, and would not resurface for decades. Until the mid-1950s, the needs of American minority groups went almost universally unaddressed. In most cases, those needs arrived out of the deliberate and oppressive nature of political institutions at all levels of government.

In this chapter, I explore the history of voting rights and political opportunities for racial minorities in the United States, the contents of the VRA including prominent amendments and judicial decisions that set the stage for multiracial coalitions, and the achievement of descriptive representation for racial minorities in Congress. I emphasize the intersection of race and the political development of the United States from the period of Reconstruction throughout the greater portion of the twentieth century. The pervasive nature and the dominance of racial orders is not the central focus, but when and where they were most prevalent within the federal context and the extent that they influenced outcomes and stifled the potential gains in racial equality remains useful for historical analysis.

The purpose of this chapter is to illustrate the highly racialized past of American political development, and how that truth has resulted in both the need for and the forging of multiracial coalitions. The historical absence of minority voices was deliberate, not simply default. Moreover, racial discrimination was prominent in all regions of country, though it manifested in various ways and targeted different groups to differing degrees. While many historians have paid close attention to the role of race in isolated periods, as well as the role of race in shaping contemporary American culture, political scientists have often obscured the continuum of racial prominence in the prioritization of policy, which in turn has led to distinctly different outcomes and life chances for members of minority groups. The consequent outcomes and opportunities (or the lack thereof) provide the foundation for multiracial coalitions today.

RACIAL ORDERS AND CONGRESSIONAL POLITICS

The dynamics of race seldom surface in accounts of American political development, though it is arguably one of the most pivotal and pervasive cleavages within the American polity. The presence of racial orders in the United States has largely gone unaddressed in historical research on legislative politics[2] and the growth of the welfare state.[3] King and Smith make the case, however, that few racially inflected contests in courts, legislatures and campaigns, and debates over policy and implementation can be understood without exploring the enduring tensions between and within that nation's racial orders (2005). In fact, many debates in US history have been influenced by political actors who can be socially located within two evolving and competing "racial institutional orders": a "white supremacist" order and an "egalitarian transformative" order (75).

To be clear, King and Smith provide an overarching definition of racial orders:

> *Racial* institutional orders are ones in which political actors have adopted (and often adapted) racial concepts, commitments, and aims in order to help bind together their coalitions and structure governing institutions that express and serve the interests of their architects ... Leaders hold them together by gaining broad agreement on the desirability of certain publicly authorized arrangements that predictably distribute power, status, and resources along what are seen as racial lines. (75)

The overt racial order of white supremacy in the South, in tandem with corresponding racial orders throughout most regions of the country, led to the continued, system-reinforced misfortune of people of color. This group status-based oppression manifested in multiple ways within the development of the American state. It did so in voice, where blacks and other groups could have benefited from indirect and direct representation, and in scheme, in that minority group attempts to participate politically were actively thwarted, and powerful governmental regimes used every means possible to render them subordinate. Denial of more immediate forms of participation through the casting of ballots rendered them powerless to elect officials of their choice. Denial of access to elected office where their needs could be voiced rendered them powerless to oppose legislation and initiatives that would worsen their predicament and perpetuate their oppression. Further, the manifestation of these racial orders pervaded all branches of government, where blacks and other minorities were openly and willfully demeaned, vilified, and subjugated by participating whites.

BLACK VOTING TRENDS AND POLITICAL OPPORTUNITIES: 1865–1957

Emancipation and Reconstruction

Prior to passage of the VRA, the voter participation of African Americans remained spotty at best. Large-scale attempts to limit black participation, most notably in the Jim Crow South, meant that black political influence was virtually nonexistent, be it on electoral outcomes or policy initiatives. While limited gains were made during the period of Reconstruction, these dwarfed the gains made during the first half of the twentieth century, when white supremacist racial orders were standard, and constant threats of brutal violence against minorities remained the norm. The years of Reconstruction exemplify the competing, evolving racial orders. In this period, the supremacist order triumphed over racial egalitarian efforts.

For the first two and a half centuries of US history, blacks, whether enslaved or free, were almost universally denied the right to vote. At certain points in the first half of the 1800s, free black men were allowed to vote in various areas of both the North and the South. However, by the time of the Civil War, free blacks were only allowed to vote in New England (with the exception of Connecticut) and New York (where a $250 fee for black voters was required). With only 6 percent of the national black population residing in New England, the actual proportion of black electoral participation was miniscule (Woodward 1966).

As early as March 1864, President Abraham Lincoln supported a limited form of suffrage for freeborn black men. After he met with two representatives of the free black community and was presented with a petition for suffrage, Lincoln wrote to Louisiana Governor (Georg) Michael Hahn: "I barely suggest for your private consideration, whether some of the colored people not be let in—as for instance, the very intelligent, and especially those who have fought gallantly in our ranks . . . But this is only a suggestion, not to the public, but to you alone" (Foner 1990, 22).

Lincoln's attempts were rebuffed by the governor, who opted not to include blacks during the Louisiana Constitutional Convention, which followed shortly thereafter. Louisiana, which had the largest free black community of the Deep South, had traditionally offered blacks more freedoms (such as traveling freely and testifying against whites in court). During the convention, slavery was abolished, but the suggestion of limited black suffrage was ignored, which in turn led to a larger split in the unionist ranks between radicals arguing for universal male suffrage, and those who opposed it. In many cases, abolitionists demanded the expulsion of all blacks from the state.

Radical Republicans at the time were primarily concerned with gaining equality before the law, not gaining suffrage. In July 1864, the Wade-Davis Bill was put forth; it would delay the start of Reconstruction until a majority of the state's white males pledged to support the Union. The bill further stated that only white males who promised that they had never aided the Confederacy should be allowed to vote. Finally, it guaranteed blacks equality before the law, but not suffrage. Pocket-vetoed by Lincoln, due to the Reconstruction efforts already commencing in Louisiana, the Wade-Davis Bill was never put into effect.

Passage of the Thirteenth Amendment in January 1865 marked a moment of both triumph and indecision. The abolition movement had successfully won the battle to dismantle slavery throughout the nation, but the question of suffrage remained. Internal struggles over whether to disband were dismissed, as the question of the vote gained prominence. Former slave Frederick Douglass was quoted as saying, "Slavery is not abolished until the black man has the ballot."

By April 11, 1865, Lincoln publicly supported black suffrage on a limited level. In his last speech, he endorsed the suffrage movement to a degree, stating that his preference would be to grant the right to vote to blacks who were "very intelligent" and serving in the Union army. Four days later, Lincoln was assassinated (Foner 1990, 33).

The new President, Andrew Johnson, did not share many of Lincoln's views. He did not seek retribution from the secessionist states; rather, he pardoned the Southern rebels and returned their confiscated property (Palmer 1998). A former Tennessee slave owner, Johnson held views on black political participation that were unfavorable, claiming blacks had less "capacity for government than any other race of people. No independent government of any form has ever been successful in their hands. On the contrary, wherever they have been left to their own devices they have shown a constant tendency to relapse into barbarism."

Later that year, many of the provisional state legislatures established by President Andrew Johnson adopted "black codes," a series of laws designed to limit the behaviors of the newly freed blacks and perpetuate their status as a subordinate labor force. In Mississippi and South Carolina, free blacks were required to sign labor contracts at the beginning of each year. Failure to enter into contract would lead to a vagrancy charge. If they broke the contract, they lost their wages and were liable for arrest by any white person. Louisiana and Texas sought to force "all members of the family" back to work, in an effort to get women who had left the fields back into them (Palmer). Black orphans were seized and apprenticed to whites, convicts were parceled out to white farmers, and any sign of black vagrancy led to work assignments for the planters. The codes also limited the areas in which blacks could purchase or rent property. Blacks were not allowed to testify in court except in cases that involved members of their race. Fines were imposed for absence from work, violation of curfew, possession of firearms, insulting gestures and acts, and seditious speech (Franklin 1994, 225).

The post-Civil War era produced some changes in the position of blacks, particularly those in the South, but it also highlighted the precarious relationship between the President and Congress, and between state legislatures and the Congress. Starting in February 1866, with the introduction of the first civil rights bill, legislation was brought by Senator Lyman Trumbull to define all persons born in the United States (with the exception of American Indians) as national citizens and grant them equal rights without regard to race. The bill also struck down the black codes, emphasizing the right for blacks to "full and equal benefit of all laws and proceedings for the security of person and property as is enjoyed by white citizens" (Palmer, 7).

President Johnson opted to veto the bill, suggesting that it discriminated against whites by providing "for the security of the colored race safeguards which go infinitely beyond any that the General Government has ever provided for the white race." This opinion was exceedingly popular among whites, who did not view blacks as their fellow citizens (Palmer). Congress passed the civil rights bill over his veto that April.

The relationship between Congress and President Johnson continued in turbulence over the next year, lending to the passage of further legislation geared toward federal control in the south. The Reconstruction Act of 1867 divided the Confederate states (with the exception of Tennessee) into five separate military districts, with martial law to prevail in each. These states were forced to create state constitutions acceptable to Congress (in this case acceptability required universal male suffrage), and no state would be admitted until it ratified the Fourteenth Amendment. Johnson vetoed this piece of legislation as well, claiming it was unconstitutional, unfair, and that blacks had not asked to vote and did not understand what the franchise was. In response, Congress overrode the veto, and enacted further legislation to reconstruct the south (Franklin 226).

State constitutions drawn up in 1867–1868 by multiracial delegations were remarkably progressive, abolishing property requirements for voting or holding office, as well as imprisonment for debt. Each of the constitutional delegations abolished slavery and many eliminated racial distinctions for laws related to property. The franchise was granted to all men in each state, with the exception of certain confederates (Franklin 238).

In February 1869, Congress approved the Fifteenth Amendment which specifically prohibited deprivation of the vote on racial grounds. Ratification of the amendment occurred in 1870. Though it granted Congress power to enforce the amendment with legislation, stronger versions that would have preempted later efforts to curtail black participation were rejected. Thus, the voting rights of black men were provided constitutional protection in technicality, but the potential for further discriminatory practices were not effectively put in check. It was anticipated that strong resistance to black voter participation would surface following the amendment, and for that reason combined with other factors, this weaker version served as a compromise.

Southern Democrats took the Fifteenth Amendment to be the crowning act of the Radical Republicans, who they felt were doing everything within their power to create black equality, grant black suffrage, and submerge states' rights (Foner 192). The Amendment, however, said nothing of the right to hold office, nor did it protect the right to vote from various literacy, educational, and property tests. Employed a few decades later, and for the good portion of eight decades, these tests would not be explicitly racial in their administration, but their adoption would further allow black disenfranchisement to continue.

The emergence of the Knights of the Ku Klux Klan also discouraged blacks from voting during the Reconstruction period and well beyond. Founded in Tennessee in 1866, it was widely known that organization members would use intimidation and brutal force as a means to deprive blacks of political equality. Representing an especially barbaric form of white domination, blacks were threatened and often run out of their communities if they insisted upon voting. Those who stayed were beaten, maimed, and hanged. In multiple instances, black elected officials were instructed to resign, lest they suffer "retributive justice" upon failure to comply. That justice was often achieved under the cover of dark, and with the collusion of various authorities.

During the Reconstruction period, Congress took an active role in the protection of various rights gained by people of color, not only in the provision thereof. In response to white vigilance, Congress enacted a series of Enforcement Acts in 1870 and 1871 to counteract terrorist violence, forbade state officials from discriminating against voters along the lines of race, and appointed election supervisors to monitor for fraud and initiate federal court cases. The Ku Klux Klan Act of 1871 brought certain crimes committed by individuals under federal jurisdiction. If states failed to prosecute conspirators who denied citizens the right to vote, hold office, serve on juries, and enjoy equal protection, federal attorneys would pursue legal redress. By that time, the limited presence of armed forces in the South proved incapable of effectively enforcing the Fifteenth Amendment or curtailing the white violent resistance that materialized.

Access to the franchise had a considerable impact on black political participation on multiple levels. Blacks now had a voice (albeit small) in the political affairs of their municipalities, their states, and their country. Electoral participation translated into gains in political office and the potential for racial uplift on a much larger scale. Blacks were also able to gain descriptive representation with officials that shared lived experiences with their constituents, and could better reflect that in attempts to limit or expand policies that affected black communities.

Even the smallest inroads led to increased opportunity for gains in political influence. With only limited access to the franchise, political leadership in the black community surfaced. Despite white supremacist terrorism, a number of black leaders continued to emerge out of their communities, taking bold initiative by voicing ideas and running for elected office. Bolstered by community institutions such as churches and schools, these leaders rose to great heights in local governments, state legislatures, and the United States Congress. Once in office, they took part in enacting laws, enforcing laws, and presenting new policy alternatives to their white peers—initiatives that often reflected the needs of black communities.

The role of indigenous institutions in the black society cannot be understated in the quest for influence and self-determination. The church played a prominent role in both the emergence and the continuation of black politics, with a number of ministers and clergymen reaching office. As a center of most black communities, and one of the few places where blacks were allowed to congregate in sizable numbers, the church was in many ways the only social institution controlled by black men. Often the only literate members of black communities, they served as election registrars and as candidates for various elected offices (Foner, 41).

Teachers, with their more advanced educational backgrounds, also assumed leadership roles within black communities. At least seventy black teachers served as state legislators during Reconstruction. Others were linked to education through the financing of schools. Like other sectors, there was a class divide, in that most of the black teachers turned elected officials had been free prior to emancipation, thus better able to pursue an education (Foner, 44).

Blacks held the greatest political influence in the state of South Carolina (Franklin, 239). In the first legislative session during Reconstruction, there were eighty-seven blacks and forty whites. Two black men served as lieutenant governor (Alonzo J. Ransier in 1870 and Richard H. Gleaves in 1872), and another two black men served as speaker of the house (Samuel J. Lee in 1872 and Roger B. Elliott in

1874). Francis Cardozo served both as secretary of state (1868–1872) and treasurer (1872–1876).

Political gains were also had in Louisiana and Mississippi, where blacks served as lieutenant governors in both states during Reconstruction, as well as members of the state legislature. Though blacks did not dominate the political realm, they were able to exert substantial political influence in the legislative arena and often sought to improve conditions in a more inclusive way (Franklin, 240).

In Georgia and Alabama, more difficulty arose in securing and maintaining political influence. In Georgia, elected black legislators were declared ineligible from participation, though they were later granted eligibility following intervention from the state supreme court. Though blacks served in both houses of the legislature in Alabama, they lacked the numbers to secure influential positions that could have led to substantive change.

Participation in legislative politics at the federal level was also highly complicated. Though the twenty blacks in the House of Representatives and two blacks in the Senate advanced a number of noteworthy endeavors, many of the bills introduced by black members did not gain passage. Similarly, many black members were unable to enjoy the prestige of committee chairmanships, along with the respect and comraderie of their white colleagues.

During Reconstruction, both black voters and black elected officials strongly supported the Republican Party. The Republicans adopted the cause of blacks for many reasons, not the least of which were expediency and strategy. To ensure their political power following the emancipation of blacks nationwide, it seemed prudent to further grant blacks the franchise and thus ensure future political success through the enlistment of loyal voters. The widespread recruitment of blacks into the Republican Party in the South continued throughout the Reconstruction period.

The inclusion of blacks in the political arena, both through a sizable voting base and the presence of elected officials, meant an increased amount of support for civil rights, most notably at the federal level. Bolstered by additional congressional action, including the Federal Civil Rights Act of 1875, Southern blacks tested their rights in railroads, steamboats, hotels, theaters, and other public accommodations. On the whole, however, blacks were not aggressive in pressing their rights, largely to avoid rebuff, insult, and potential violence. Whites, in turn, often withdrew from desegregated facilities or, at the least, limited their patronage of such facilities (Woodward 1966).

At the same time, the judicial system did its fair share in unraveling the civil rights gains made through legislation during the decade of 1865 to 1875. Though never the advocate for blacks prior to emancipation, the system became a staunch ally to white planters after the Civil War, helping to undo what was lost during the war. In many ways, the courts never grew willing to recognize blacks as anything other than disposable property. Citizenship, and the privileges that would accompany that status, would not be protected by the courts during the nineteenth century. In *United States v. Reese* (1875),[4] the US Supreme Court declared that the Fifteenth Amendment did not protect the right to vote for anyone; rather, it merely prevented racial preference of one over another in conferring that right. In *United States v. Cruikshank* (1875),[5] the Supreme Court ruled the Enforcement Act of 1870 unconstitutional because it covered more offenses than were punishable under the Fifteenth Amendment.

The resistance to peaceful coexistence among blacks and whites was ever present. Racial clashes were the norm in states like Louisiana, South Carolina, and Mississippi. Conservative Democrats organized "White Leagues" and plotted to overthrow the Radical Republican government in Louisiana. In South Carolina, black militiamen were arrested on a false charge of blocking traffic during a July 4th parade in 1876. Once arrested, they were killed by angry whites. The Republican Party in Mississippi was all but dissolved by 1875, after a period in which the state was on the verge of war. Governor Adelbert Ames maintained a black militia that whites took increasing offense to, resulting in the private assemblage of a white militia. Though Ames promised to disband the black militia, chaos and killings remained the norm.

The end of Reconstruction also marked the end of the political goals achieved by and for blacks during the decade following the Civil War. By 1876, many of the Radical Republicans of the North had grown tired of championing the rights of blacks, and the racial order of white supremacy won out. In the South, violence and mayhem rocked the shaky foundations of politics and society, as racial tension and hatred grew increasingly charged.

THE DOMINATION OF JIM CROW

The prevalence of Jim Crow came into full force following the end of Reconstruction. During this time, it became increasingly clear that blacks would be disenfranchised in the South, and that a life of peonage and state-sanctioned inequality was in store for them. The term "Jim Crow" was an adjective in popular use as early as 1838, in reference to the subjugation of blacks in the South, most notably manifested in the segregation statutes and discriminatory policies that served as constant and public reminders of the inferior societal position of blacks. Laws sanctioned the racial ostracism that extended into almost all aspects of life: churches, educational facilities, housing, employment, and dining, among others. The requirements of the codes that existed after Reconstruction strongly resembled codes that existed during slavery, but with at least one great exception: during slavery, there was a relative laxity that mitigated the harshness of the black codes. After the end of Reconstruction, the codes were strictly enforced, and extended all the way to hospitals, orphanages, prisons, and even cemeteries (Woodward 1966).

The legislative assault on black political gains made during Reconstruction came shortly and swiftly after the Compromise of 1877. According to Harvard Sitkoff, "Congress permitted the white south to reduce blacks to a state of peonage, to disregard their civil rights, and to disenfranchise them by force, intimidation and statute. So did the Supreme Court" (1993, 4). Effectively invalidating the Fourteenth and Fifteenth Amendments of the Constitution, all three branches of the federal government exercised their ability to limit the growth of black political power and access to opportunity. In effect, there were many avenues of oppression that racist whites took to further black subordination long after the dissolution of slavery.

The Compromise, which marked the end of the Reconstruction period, required all federal troops to withdraw from the South, federal patronage for the South, at least one Southern Democratic cabinet member, and subsidies for internal improvements. In return, Republican Presidential candidate Rutherford Hayes assumed office in the White House, despite his loss of the popular vote to Governor Samuel Tilden of New York. Hayes, who had pledged protection of the rights of Southern blacks, moderated his position after taking office, endorsing "wise, honest, and peaceful local self-government." Most pertinent to blacks, the removal of the troops signaled the tacit agreement between the federal government and white Southerners that blacks could be dealt with as deemed necessary. As in many instances, the resolution of this particular political conflict came at the expense of the black population. Soon thereafter, multiple disenfranchising conventions were held in the South, resulting in revisions of various state constitutions. Whereas blacks had elected 324 black officials to legislatures and Congress in 1872, by the year 1900, only five were in place.

The last two decades of the nineteenth century gave rise to state-sanctioned racial discrimination, from which emerged a vicious racial caste system. Various obstacles were put into place in effort to dissolve black political participation and any form of interracial alliance altogether (Davidson, 11). Along with voter fraud and the threat of violence, blacks were subject to literacy tests, white-only primary elections, and many other forms of political exclusion.

The end of Reconstruction also served as a precursor to significant changes in statewide voting procedures in the South. Though racist Southern whites vehemently opposed the progressive state constitutions of 1867 and 1868, given the chance, the only major provisions they sought to undo post-Reconstruction were the black enfranchisement clauses (Franklin, 238). Florida adopted a new constitution in 1885. Soon thereafter, Mississippi, South Carolina, Louisiana, and Virginia followed suit.

The political exclusion of blacks, particularly in the South, was to their detriment through direct and indirect means. Their direct inability to participate through voting and holding office meant they were wholly powerless to prevent the hate and bigotry of supremacists from running

rampant. Excluded from these bodies of government, venomous discriminatory policies emerged out of state legislatures, only to be further
sustained by the courts. The 1880s marked the advent of legally sanctioned segregation on public transportation. Tennessee started the trend,
with Florida, Mississippi, Texas, and Louisiana following by 1890. The
Carolinas and Virginia were not far behind.

In terms of voter deterrence, Mississippi was the first to develop legally
defensible measures to remove black voters from the electoral rolls. In
1890, it adopted a state constitution that directed disqualification measures
toward blacks. Among these included two-year residency requirements
(blacks were more transient than whites for various reasons), a test on specific provisions of the Constitution that satisfied the registrar, and a poll
tax of $2, with presentation of a receipt required on Election Day. In addi-
tion, men who had committed crimes such as fraud, arson, and theft (pre-
sumably committed more by blacks) were restricted from the polls, while
murderers and rapists were not excluded (Palmer). In the end, all but two
Southern states implemented literacy tests as a means of black exclusion.

Louisiana, with its implementation of a new constitution, including
the "grandfather clause" in 1898, was remarkably successful in purging
potential black voters from the rolls. These were used largely to exempt
poor whites from passing literacy tests as a requirement of voting participation, to which blacks were still subject. The number of blacks on
the electoral rolls went from 130,344 in 1896 to 5,320 in 1900 (Palmer,
41; Franklin, 261). The device, which required that the permanent voter
list consist of men whose fathers and grandfathers were qualified to vote
in 1867, drew stark lines along the racial divide. Despite opposition from
black lawmakers and public figures at the time, the newly designed constitutions of the South presented a rigid, dichotomous system: white and
black, privileged and powerless. In 1915, the Supreme Court declared the
"grandfather clause" unconstitutional.[6]

Strategies of minority vote dilution and political exclusion were rigor-
ously imposed by state and local officials, most prominently in the South,
where black populations were the highest. Though the Great Migration
(which began roughly in the 1910s) led to demonstrable changes in the

geographic distribution of blacks throughout the United States, especially to large Northern cities, the majority remained in the South, ensconced in the labor force and with little or no social, economic, or political influence to speak of.

Violence was, by and large, the most effective means of prohibiting black political participation. In countless communities, blacks were not allowed to enter town on Election Day, under the threat of severe retaliation (Franklin). More generally, election officials deliberately located polling places far from black communities, often with road blocks and other logistical hurdles put in place during election time. In other cases, officials changed polling locations at the last minute, with no notification for black voters. In some instances, blacks were notified of a location change that never took place.

The political arm of the Jim Crow laws, including but not limited to literacy tests, recitation of the Constitution, and property ownership, were often designed with the express intent of preventing black access to the franchise. County and state legislators often manipulated redistricting processes and suffrage restrictions as a means to curtail black involvement in the political process. The legislatures and other governing bodies were almost wholly controlled by zealous white supremacist Democrats, who used poll taxes, confusing election schemes, and complicated balloting processes as means to exclude blacks. In addition, long lists of infractions were created that could qualify as "suffrage disqualifications," including minor crimes such as petty larceny.

The post-Reconstruction party politics of the antebellum South presented two starkly different alternatives, neither of which was entirely palatable to (let alone in the best interests of) the black community. On the one hand, blacks were presented with the Republicans, who had all but abandoned them in the Compromise of 1877, after portraying themselves as the social conscience of the nation, while blacks were merely wards of the state. On the other hand, conservative Democrats made paternalistic arguments regarding blacks, arguing against both their participation and autonomy, and in favor of measures that limited their mobility within most all circles of life.

The emergence and attractiveness of the populist movement among the black community was highly pragmatic. Populists argued against the Southern economic structures and capitalism that fed off institutions such as slavery and other varied forms of servitude. Instead, they focused on a common cause and a common oppressor who perpetuated poverty and inequality (Woodward 1966). By 1892, resurgent farmers of the South, both black and white, were united through similar economic conditions and stood by the Populist platform of political equality. Newfound interracial alliances between whites and blacks that developed in the Populist Party were met with staunch resistance from the Democrats, with at least fifteen black populists killed in Georgia during the state elections of 1892 (Franklin, 258).

The Supreme Court continued its substantial role in the reversal of Reconstruction gains and the return to white dominance. In 1883, the courts struck down the Civil Rights Act of 1875 and blacks were banned from white hotels, barbershops, theaters, and restaurants (Franklin, 262). Though most Southern states had laws banning interracial marriage and segregating schools by 1885, these measures were challenged. In turn, the Court firmly upheld segregation in 1896, in the case of *Plessy v. Ferguson*,[7] claiming that policies of separation by racial background did not constitute unequal treatment, thus they were not in violation of the Constitution.

By 1910, the vast majority of African American men were disenfranchised,[8] though small numbers continued to vote. Interested black voters were plagued with schemes designed with the purpose of their exclusion, among them unfair examinations, intimidation, and delaying the registration process until the deadline had passed. In the 1920s, black voters often found that their names were not on the list of voters, that their names had mistakenly been placed on the white voters list, or that their names or addresses appeared differently on the list from that on their certificates—all of which were technicalities that served as disqualifications.[9]

The exclusion experienced by blacks was well known, widespread, and enforced by Southern whites. In 1927, Senator Cole Blease of South Carolina addressed the right to suffrage, boldly admitting that the purpose of the 1895 State Constitution was to prohibit voting among African

Americans. In regard to the 1922 Presidential election, won by Calvin Coolidge, Blease noted, "I think Mr. Coolidge received 1100 votes in my state. I do not know where he got them. I was astonished to know that they were cast and shocked to know they were counted."[10]

Black migration to Northern cities such as New York, Chicago, Detroit, and St. Louis resulted in increased, but limited, representation in the US Congress during the late 1920s and throughout the 1930s. In 1900, only 10 percent of blacks in the US lived in the North or the West, which effectively eliminated them as a political force. Changes in geographic distribution of blacks, to the extreme aggravation and wrath of the Southern planter elite, resulted in increased political participation at both the local and federal levels.

Between the years of 1910 and 1960, the distribution of the black population changed substantially. The out-migration of the black community from the South to other regions of the United States led to sizable populations and communities that could amass political influence elsewhere. During those five decades, the nationwide total black population increased by 92 percent. The number of African Americans outside the South increased by more than 500 percent. Meanwhile, in the South, the number of blacks increased by only 29 percent, reflecting the black rejection of oppressive Southern regimes (McAdam 1982).

The political significance of the out-migration from the South was monumental, in that black opportunity was not stymied and checked at anywhere near the rate that occurred in the Jim Crow South. As the numbers increased, for the first time in the twentieth century, Chicago sent a black representative to Washington, DC to serve in the house. Oscar De Priest, a Republican, represented black interests in profound ways. During his three terms (1929–1935) he introduced multiple anti-discrimination bills to Congress, including a 1933 amendment barring discrimination in the Civilian Conservation Corps, which was passed in both houses and signed into law by President Roosevelt. He also introduced anti-lynching legislation and proposed that those who believed that they could not get a fair trial due to racial background be permitted to transfer to another jurisdiction. Though ultimately unsuccessful, these bills demonstrated his commitment to breaking down the barriers of discrimination.

De Priest's downfall, however, seemed to be his lack of attention to the needs of the poor, and black poverty was very much a reality in his district. He consistently opposed federal aid to the needy following the advent of the Depression. His defeat came with the rise of the "Roosevelt Republicans," that is, Republicans who repeatedly and in large numbers voted for Democrats and their progressive poverty agenda. Defeated by Arthur Mitchell, a Republican-turned-Democrat, in 1934 and again in 1936, Mitchell continued much of De Priest's work on anti-discrimination legislation, while still supporting the more liberal fiscal policies of the New Deal. Mitchell served through 1942.

The elections of De Priest and Mitchell in Chicago marked a substantive difference between North and South, one that would grow more prominent in the following decades. The combination of multiple factors, including Southern oppression, economic opportunity in industrialized cities in the North, and consequent black migration from the South to the North, all contributed to a changing dynamic in minority influence in the political process. Though the transition was gradual, every accomplishment signified a changing political landscape and growing opportunity for advancement.

THE 1940S AND 1950S

The differences between black political participation in the North and the South became more prominent as the nation moved toward the midpoint of the twentieth century. Advances made in either region were often hard fought, and inclusion remained limited at best. With notable exceptions in the North, blacks were almost completely shut out of legislative politics at the federal level. The black community gained few electoral successes, and even fewer policies to address their social and economic conditions. The Supreme Court did make a small number of decisions, ruling against the voting exclusion of blacks in the South and the institutions that promoted such policies, but in essence the decades of the 1940s and 1950s were continuations of political, social, and economic oppression that had already molded the black experience in the United States for centuries.

The few electoral gains made by African Americans extended into the 1940s. William Dawson, a black Democrat from the south side of Chicago, was elected to Congress in 1942. Meanwhile, Adam Clayton Powell from New York was elected in 1944. The addition of Charles C. Diggs, Jr., in 1954 marked the first time in the twentieth century that three blacks served in Congress.

The *de jure* segregation of the South, combined with the extensive voting provisions designed to disenfranchise minorities, translated to absolutely zero black representation from the South at the federal level. Schemes to intimidate and further marginalize minority voters were widespread and virulent. One man, a coal miner born in 1910, wrote of his experience trying to register to vote in Alabama during the 1940s:

At that particular time I went up to the county courthouse to the board of registrars. I walked in and the registrar was in there. He started washing his hands. He washed his hands until two white people came in, and he dried his hands off and came and waited on them. Then, he went right back to washing his hands again. Finally, he came and just like this he said: "What you want boy?" I said, "I wants to register to vote." So he got out a registration form and laid it out there before me and I tried to figure it out. He came back and looked at it, balled it up and threw it in the wastebasket. All he said was "You disqualified, you didn't answer the question." (Chafe et al. 2001)

Restrictions on black voter registration were seldom checked, and often willfully encouraged by the dominant white supremacist power structures in place at the time. White officials repeatedly disqualified blacks for spelling and technical errors on registration applications. In many cases, voter registration offices limited their hours of operation as a means to deter black voters as they sought their inclusion in the franchise.

Attempts to gain influence through federal statute were repeatedly thwarted, as efforts to abolish the poll tax were defeated on multiple occasions and states kept in place the literacy tests and the various forms of intimidation that bolstered white dominance throughout the South (Woodward 141). Indeed, the outright dismissal of blacks who desired to vote was commonplace, as was the threat of violence that accompanied the attempt to claim the right to vote. Repercussions for such behavior included the risk of losing their jobs, their homes, and even their lives (Sitkoff 1993).

Fraudulent election-day practices also bolstered white dominance in the Southern states. The practice of stuffing ballot boxes was both prevalent and unchecked. With no uniform ballot, white Democratic voters often made up hundreds of extra ballots for their cause. Similarly, ballot-counting revealed remarkable inaccuracies and manipulation among local registrars. In many cases, white and black Republicans outnumbered Democrats at the polls, but the Democrats prided themselves on "outcounting" the opposition (Franklin, 255).

Like most sectors of society, white-only practices remained widespread in United States politics throughout the first six decades of the twentieth century, although court rulings gradually struck them down. In 1944, the Supreme Court struck down the white-only primary of the Texas State Democratic Party in *Smith v. Allwright*.[11] Though the democrats made efforts to turn their party into a private club in order to limit membership, the courts refused to uphold any party rules that excluded blacks on the basis that the delegation of the authority *by* the state may make the party's actions the action *of* the state.[12]

The court decisions, particularly those abolishing the white-only primaries, did result in increased black participation. In 1940, roughly 2 percent of the black voting age population in twelve Southern states actually qualified to vote. By 1947, 12 percent (more than 600,000 black citizens) were qualified and by 1952, roughly 1.2 million blacks were qualified to vote in the South, representing slightly less than a quarter of the black voting age population.

The results in the voter registration gains were pronounced. Said C. Vann Woodward, "For the first time since the beginning of the century Negroes reappeared in elective and appointive office, largely in the upper South, on school boards, city councils and other minor posts" (142). But the gains held in the upper South did not extend to those blacks in the lower South, where little change in voter registration and office-holding occurred. The limited gains that were made were somewhat undone with the rise of militant Southern resistance. Said Woodward, "In many Black Belt counties it was apparent that so long as voter registration and poll supervision were entrusted entirely to local authority there would be little hope for significant Negro participation in the most elementary political rights" (142).

In Tuskegee, Alabama, the boundary lines of the sizable city were redrawn, in an effort to exclude all but ten of its black residents, though blacks constituted a considerable majority in the late 1950s. The Supreme Court struck down this measure in *Gomillion v. Lightfoot* (1960),[13] when it was charged that this new districting plan violated the equal protection clause of the Fourteenth Amendment, as well as the Fifteenth Amendment. Prior to this point, the courts had not intervened in the districting policies of state and local governments.

In all, the persistence of Southern white resistance to federal law drastically complicated the process of acquiring political influence for African Americans. Though the majority of political successes were achieved through the judicial system, the courts had no means to enforce their decisions. By the late 1950s, disenfranchisement continued to prevail in the Jim Crow South, despite numerous court rulings. Though civil rights organizations put forth intensive efforts—most notably the National Association for the Advancement of Colored People (NAACP) and the Southern Christian Leadership Conference (SCLC)—and achieved victories in the courts and in Congress, still fewer than one in four blacks of voting age in the South could vote.

REFORM, TURMOIL, AND CHANGE: 1957–1965

The period of time immediately preceding passage of the VRA was notably turbulent, due in large part to increased resistance to the civil rights movement. Any number of factors contributed to the growth of political opportunity for blacks and other minorities, including a growing network of organizations dedicated to institutional reform and policy change, a shifting political climate both in Washington and among the American public at large, and multiple court decisions that balanced the playing field and reduced the ability of state and municipal governments to limit and dilute voting power.

For the first time since Reconstruction, Congress enacted civil rights legislation in 1957, declaring the disenfranchisement of blacks illegal. With the purpose of protecting black voting rights, the Civil Rights Act of 1957 authorized the Attorney General of the United States to bring about lawsuits to protect voting rights and hold persons in violation in criminal contempt. The Act also provided for the appointment of an Assistant Attorney General to lead a Civil Rights Division in the Department of Justice. In addition, it required that special three-judge federal district courts be convened, with jurisdiction over civil rights cases taken out of the state courts by the Department of Justice. Finally, it created a Commission on Civil Rights to gather information on voting discrimination. Unfortunately, the act proved ineffective due to various hurdles. Nationwide hearings conducted by the Civil Rights Commission were extremely lengthy, and the legal tactics used to delay the process resulted in only four cases being heard and decided in the three years following passage of the Act.

With the desire to strengthen the prior legislation, Congress enacted the Civil Rights Act of 1960. States were additionally held responsible for the application of racist registration policies, not just local registrars. Federal referees were authorized to register qualified voters and investigate complaints of racial discrimination in voting processes. The Act further required voting records to be preserved for twenty-two months following any primary, special, or general election where there were candidates for a federal office. A federal district judge was empowered to issue registration orders and to replace state registrars with federal officials.[14]

Though vastly improved from its predecessor, the Civil Rights Act of 1960 was not without its shortcomings. The burden of proof fell upon often-disadvantaged black citizens, who were required to initiate legal action in already hostile environments. By 1963, the Civil Rights Commission concluded that the federal government should assume this role, lessening the burden on black citizens, who routinely lacked the resources to challenge each and every individual case of systemic racism. The approach to vote discrimination through litigation was proving both time-consuming and ineffective, and showed no noticeable increase in black voter registration.

Though many officials seemed rather wedded to the litigious approach of addressing voter grievances, the intensifying climate surrounding race relations, combined with outbursts of violence notably in the South, seemed to sway them in favor of more preemptive federal enforcement of voter protection. Passage of the Civil Rights Act of 1964 was largely in response to repressive violence in Birmingham, Alabama and Philadelphia, Mississippi. The legislation contained voting provisions that attempted to expedite vote discrimination court hearings, allowed for temporary registrars, and forbade local officials from applying standards to some registrants (i.e., black registrants) but not to others (i.e., white registrants). It also provided for a presumption of literacy in any voting rights court case where the voter applicant had completed sixth grade in an accredited, English-speaking school.[15] These efforts still proved ineffective, as state or local jurisdictions would often pass or enforce different laws and regulations as means of circumventing court orders issued during the litigation process.

In addition to the many vote-based achievements of the act, the Civil Rights Act of 1964 established a federal Equal Opportunity Employment Commission, while also extending the Commission on Civil Rights. It provided the Attorney General with additional power to protect citizens against both segregation policies and discrimination in voting, education, and the use of public facilities. Moreover, it required the elimination of discrimination in federally assisted programs. State and local governments that failed to comply would have funding withheld by the federal government. These notable successes empowered minority communities, many of whom were still struggling to gain influence in the political system.

Multiple court cases preceded the VRA, increasing the political power of ethnic minorities in terms of electoral participation and focusing on fairness in apportionment and redistricting processes. Three pivotal cases, in conjunction with the statutes passed by Congress and signed into law, set the foundation for the VRA and further protection of minority voters, both by setting a precedent in which the courts could intervene in the reapportionment process, and by setting boundaries for states that sought to disenfranchise and dilute minority votes.

In *Baker v. Carr* (1962),[16] the Supreme Court ruled that the disproportionate concentration of citizens, especially minorities, in large cities must be reflected in legislative district boundaries in the state of Tennessee. The sixty-year-old state benchmark plan provided greater proportional representation to residents of rural areas, resulting in the dilution of urban and minority votes. In most cases, the only blacks allowed to vote were city dwellers, but urban and suburban areas were drastically underrepresented in legislative boundary designs. Moreover, the decision established court jurisdiction in the matter of redistricting processes. The state of Tennessee made the argument that this situation was a political, state-based matter that did not and should not require federal intervention. With the declaration by the Supreme Court that reapportionment matters were justiciable (and not to be left to state governments without oversight), the stage was set for further imposition from the courts.

Soon thereafter the Warren Court handed down the *Reynolds v. Sims* (1964)[17] decision. With eight justices providing support, the court found that state legislative districts had to be roughly equal in terms of population. In what has come to be known as the "One man, one vote" decision, the court ruled against unequal districting that empowered small numbers of individuals over large masses. Said Chief Justice Earl Warren in the majority opinion, "Legislators represent people, not trees or acres. Legislators are elected by voters, not farms or cities or economic interests." This principle was extended later that year to congressional district plans in *Wesberry v. Sanders*.[18]

Political influence often surfaced in the form of powerful alliances, with perhaps the greatest ally of the civil rights movement being President

Lyndon B. Johnson. Executive implementation of both the Civil Rights Act of 1964 and the VRA of 1965 was swift and uncompromising during the Johnson Administration (Woodward 1966), and Johnson himself played a pivotal role in the passage of both acts. A former United States Senator from Texas, Johnson was very familiar with the power struggles and internal politics of the legislative branch. Enactment of both pieces of landmark legislation required Johnson's strong will and calculated manner.

THE VRA OF 1965

Congress passed the VRA in 1965 with the strong support of President Johnson after the March 1965 Bloody Sunday event in Alabama. The Senate passed a version with 77 Senators in favor and 19 against. In the House, there were 333 members in support, 85 against. The majority of those voting against the bill were Southern white Democrats, who clung to racist political practices and resisted all change that would erode their power. Johnson signed the bill into law on August 6, 1965. Subsequent amendments were passed in 1970, 1975, 1982, 1992, and 2006 to better meet the changing needs for protection.

The provisions of the VRA remained somewhat vague, in that they were unclear about how to successfully achieve the goals delineated. While it was clear that the Act was put forth as a means to enforce the Fifteenth Amendment, the wording of the Act did not offer strict guidelines detailing, among other things, the logistics of reaching that goal, though it did specify a more prominent and preemptive role on the part of the federal government as well as a trigger formula to determine the most egregious culprits of vote suppression. The major provisions of the VRA of 1965 (as amended) are as follows:

1. Prohibit the enactment of any election law to deny or abridge voting rights on account of race or color;
2. Suspend all literacy tests in states and counties that used them and where less than 50 percent of adults had voted in 1964;

3. Prohibit the enforcement of new voting rules or practices until
   federal reviewers determine if their use would continue voting
   discrimination;
4. Assign federal examiners to list qualified applicants to vote
   and to serve as poll watchers;
5. Authorize the Attorney General to institute civil actions to
   seek enforcement of the act;
6. Provide election materials and oral assistance if a sizable percentage of the political jurisdiction were of a single language
   minority, and
7. Prohibit any person acting under color of law or otherwise
   from intimidating or denying *any* eligible person from voting.

Sections 2 and 5 were of particular importance. Section 2 generally
prohibited practices that led to minority vote dilution, and thus fewer
chances for minorities to elect representatives of their choice throughout
the nation. All jurisdictions—municipal, state, and federal—are subject
to compliance with Section 2. It provided a more normative prescription
for minority political achievement, prohibiting any voting qualification
or prerequisite to voting, or any standard practice or procedure imposed
by any state or subdivision that results in the denial or abridgement of the
right to vote based on race, color, or membership in a language minority.[19]

Section 5 was more punitive in its thrust. It expressly required specific
areas ("covered jurisdictions") to obtain approval for new districting procedures from either the Attorney General or the US District Court for the
District of Columbia. The language of the Act, specifically Section 5, did
make clear that the voting procedures "not have the purpose" and "not
have the effect of denying or abridging the right to vote on the account of
race or color." But the VRA required more than procedural requirements
that individuals must observe in order to vote. The law required oversight
for every change in election law in a covered jurisdiction, to the dismay of
many of the jurisdictions at hand.

The determination of jurisdictions that would be "covered" by the
VRA arrived out of a coverage formula delineated in Section 4. Federal

intervention in state and local regulation of the electoral process was limited to jurisdictions where there was evidence that racially discriminatory voting procedures had taken place. This evidence manifested as the result of a coverage formula adopted to determine which states and political subdivisions should be covered by the Act. Low registration and voting statistics in jurisdictions that required literacy tests and other devices were assumed to be discriminatory in effect. The following jurisdictions were covered by the triggering formula of Section 4(b) of the VRA in 1965: Alabama, Georgia, Louisiana, Mississippi, South Carolina, Virginia, thirty-nine counties in North Carolina, and specified counties in Arizona and Hawaii.

South Carolina, however, was the first state to challenge the constitutionality of the VRA. In 1966, the state argued that the legislation far exceeded the constitutional authority of Congress.[20] Chief Justice Earl Warren rejected each of the state's claims, upholding every provision of the statute and further emphasizing the broad means by which Congress could choose to enforce the Fifteenth Amendment and the prohibition of racial discrimination in the right to vote.

The confluence of support from the Presidency, Congress, and the Supreme Court was crucial in the struggle to overcome the white supremacist racial order that had dominated American politics for centuries. The willingness of the leadership of each branch to bring sweeping change in the name of justice was unparalleled in United States history. The coalitions built and solidified during the decades preceding the 1960s, combined with the rising awareness around the country of the oppressive political schemes of the South,[21] helped to mobilize and empower those who sought to end the state-sanctioned political, economic, and social totalitarianism that had flourished in the South since the end of Reconstruction and removal of Northern troops.

Descriptive representation increased substantially following the passage of the VRA in 1965. When the VRA went into effect, only six African American Representatives served in the House,[22] none of whom were from Southern states. That number more than doubled in the next seven years with the elections of Ron Dellums, George Collins, Ralph Metcalfe,

Parren Mitchell, William Clay, Shirley Chisholm, Charles Rangel, and Louis Stokes—all of whom were also from the North, Midwest, and West. Even with the changes made through voting rights legislation, Southern legislatures remained openly hostile to the notion of creating districts where black candidates could gain office. In most cases, it would not be until the election following the 1990 census and redistricting that African Americans would be elected from Southern states.[23]

Compared to black representation in the nineteenth century, the Representatives of the civil rights era were not only from Northern states (William Lacy Clay from Missouri being an exception), but their presence represented another change in the black population: each of these legislators was from an urban area. The great migration that lasted from 1910 to 1960 bore fruit in legislative politics. Political achievements that were unattainable in the South crept up in the North, where large black communities found strength in numbers. Whereas many of the earlier representatives had arrived in office from careers as ministers and teachers, this new class was comprised of lawyers, businessmen, and state and local elected officials. Only one—Shirley Chisholm—was a teacher.

Not surprisingly, the increase in descriptive representation for blacks paralleled black voter participation. A combination of intense voter registration drives, the enactment of the VRA, and the increased awareness of African Americans about the power that existed through the ballot created a "black political revolution" in the United States (Franklin 1994, 525). In the South, black voter participation rose to 62 percent in 1968, up from 12 percent in 1947 (Alt 1994). Similarly, the number of black delegates to national political conventions increased, representing a voice in presidential candidate selection.

The rise of African American elected officials stemmed far beyond the United States Congress. In 1966, soon after enactment of the VRA, there were six black members of Congress, ninety-seven black state legislators, and no black mayors. After the Census of 1970 and the consequent redistricting, sixteen black members served in Congress and more than 200 black state legislators served in thirty-seven state legislatures. On multiple levels, the VRA signified success and broadly increased the access and potential influence of blacks.

BEYOND BLACK AND WHITE

> The fight for equality must be fought on many fronts—in the urban slums, in the sweat shops of the factories and fields. Our separate struggles are really one—a struggle for freedom, for dignity and for humanity. You and your valiant fellow workers have demonstrated your commitment to righting grievous wrongs forced upon exploited people. We are together with you in spirit and in determination that our dreams for a better tomorrow will be realized. MLK
>
> —TELEGRAM FROM MARTIN LUTHER KING,
> JR. TO CESAR CHAVEZ, *September 19, 1966*

Tremendous difficulty arises when offering even an abbreviated political history for Latinos and Asian Pacific Americans in the United States. Given the substantial variation within each pan-ethnic group, it is unwise to make overarching arguments. Latino and Asian Pacific American populations both comprise substantial internal diversity: group members originate from many different countries; there remains considerable intra-group variation in terms of the number of familial generations in the US; and there is a history in various parts of the US where these groups, along with Native Americans, were categorized as white.[24] Though commonplace in contemporary racial categorizations, the institutionalization of these pan-ethnic groups is relatively recent in US history, generally occurring within the last five decades. In this section, I emphasize the targeted "othering" of these groups by governmental entities, and the corresponding legislative and judicial protections gradually afforded them prior to their inclusion in the 1975 Amendments to the VRA.

Notable similarities exist between the black experience in the South and that of Mexican Americans in the Southwest. Similar to blacks,

Mexican Americans were also subject to brutal violence from both lynch mobs and law enforcement, the most well-documented being the Texas Rangers (Carrigan 2003). Social segregation was fairly widespread, with signs that read "No Dogs or Mexicans" in any number of public and private facilities. Mexican American children were often sent to segregated schools throughout the Southwest, until the Federal District Court of Los Angeles struck down the school segregation of Orange County, California in 1947 as unconstitutional and a violation of equal protection.[25] The Ninth Circuit Court of Appeals upheld the earlier ruling, though it did so neither on equal protection grounds, nor did it challenge the separate but equal clause of *Plessy v. Ferguson.*

One particularly fruitful multiracial political coalition surfaced at this point, with Thurgood Marshall and the NAACP (which had traditionally championed consensus issues within the African American community) supporting the Mexican plaintiffs' attempt to end school segregation. Moreover, California Governor Earl Warren (who would become Chief Justice of the United States Supreme Court six years later) quickly outlawed Mexican segregation in California schools, requiring all municipal governments, including counties and school districts, to comply. Though not required by the federal court system, changes in statute were made to the California Education Code, which at the time included provisions allowing for the separate schooling of children of "Chinese, Japanese and Mongolian" descent. Led by Governor Warren in 1947, the code was further amended to prohibit the de jure segregated education of *all* children within the state of California.

The inclusion of Mexican Americans (and all racial groups) under the equal protection clause was not firmly established until 1954 under the Warren Court, in the case of *Hernandez v. Texas,*[26] where a Mexican American man was tried and convicted by an all-white jury. In a unanimous landmark court decision, the court opined that all racial groups were covered by the equal protection clause of the Fourteenth Amendment.

Prior to this date, little if any recognition of a pan-ethnic Hispanic racial minority had occurred at the federal level, though recognition of a Mexican "race"[27] emerged in the 1930 US Census, but did not include other Spanish-speaking groups, such as Puerto Ricans, Cubans, and other groups originating in Latin America (Orozco 2009). Although anti-Mexican sentiments were prominent in the Southwest, and state and local governments had highly discriminatory policies in place, the racialization of a broad Latino category of individuals had yet to surface.

A handful of men "of Hispanic descent" were elected to Congress from Louisiana, New Mexico, Texas, and California prior to the VRA. Of those, only one Senator out of four descended from Mexico, and three Representatives out of eleven descended from Mexico. The remaining senators and representatives directly descended from European Spanish families. Until 1973 all but one Hispanic member of Congress represented districts in the Southwest, Louisiana, or California.[28] This, in part, reflects the demographic trends in the national population: the Puerto Rican population was increasing in size and prominence in New York, but had not achieved the numbers necessary for electoral success until the late 1940s and throughout the 1950s, when the mainland population surpassed 500,000. Meanwhile, the Cuban American population, located primarily in Florida, did not surpass 500,000 until 1980. As such, the overwhelming majority of early twentieth century political opportunities for Latinos prior to the VRA centered in the Southwest, which had been part of Mexico until the Treaty of Guadalupe Hidalgo in 1848.

For Asian Americans, the two largest groups prior to passage of the VRA were Chinese and Japanese, with an overwhelming majority residing in the states of California and Hawaii. Historically, the relationship between the United States government and Asian American groups has been strained. Representing the largest Asian American population in the US, roughly 100,000 Chinese immigrated to California during the nineteenth century, working mostly in the California gold rush and then in menial labor positions including railroad construction. Subject to brutal working conditions, Chinese laborers often suffered violent beatings at the hands of their superiors. By 1882, Congress passed the Chinese Exclusion Act, banning Chinese immigration. The statute remained in place through 1943, when it was replaced with a policy strictly limiting immigration.[29] Non-Chinese Asian groups were also targeted by harsh US immigration policies. In the 1920s, a series of reforms curtailed virtually all Asian immigration to the US, no longer targeting only the Chinese. These reforms remained in place through the 1960s.[30]

Like African Americans and Mexicans, Asian American children were also required to attend segregated schools in the state of California, where the majority of the immigrants settled and remain to present day. As mentioned before, schools in California were officially desegregated under the leadership of Governor Warren in 1947.

The history of Japanese Americans in the US includes tremendous tragedy, the most striking being the internment of roughly 110,000 persons of Japanese ancestry in May 1942, during World War II.[31] Authorized by President Franklin Delano Roosevelt the February prior, Executive Order 9066 allowed for the creation of internment camps, arguably devised with the purpose of preventing espionage. Taking place in the months after the Japanese attack on Pearl Harbor, many Californians were preoccupied with the potential threat of an attack on the West Coast. Those persons living near the West Coast deemed to be from enemy ancestry, regardless of their citizenship status, were relocated to internment and detention camps at least 100 miles inland from the Pacific. Anti-Japanese sentiments reached an all-time high by this point, and Japanese Americans were denied even basic protections and civil liberties. The Supreme Court upheld the use of internment camps during wartime in *Korematsu v. United States* in December 1944, but a separate ruling was offered stipulating that loyal citizens of the United States could not be detained without just cause, regardless of their cultural ancestry.

Prior to the passage of the 1975 Amendments to the VRA, only six Asian Americans had been elected to Congress, all of whom were elected from California or Hawaii, including three Japanese American men, one Japanese American woman, one Chinese American man, and one Indian American man. Though immigration numbers have increased substantially since the 1960s, particularly for Filipinos, Koreans, and Indian Americans, the exclusionary policies from the late nineteenth through the mid-twentieth century had a huge impact on the racial demographics of the United States, prioritizing Northern and Western Europeans, while turning away those from groups that did not embody the civic myth of white, Anglo-Saxon, Protestant males.

The 1975 Amendments

Though the initial version of the VRA protected the right to vote for all citizens regardless of race or color, the primary focus of concern was on the African American community. Black participation and efforts to exclude black politicians from elected office were the central emphasis of voting rights discourse. Meanwhile, certain state and local governments employed alternative means to continue the targeted exclusion of a wide range of ethnic groups. Not until the early 1970s did the federal legislature directly acknowledge the attempts of state and local governments to limit the political participation of Latinos, Asian Americans, and Native Americans through various means, including the manipulation of prominent language barriers. Holding numerous hearings between 1970 and 1975, the testimonies of members from these various groups led to congressional action to amend the VRA on behalf of language minorities.[32]

At the congressional hearings, Puerto Rican and Chicano citizens testified about voting experiences and candidacy hurdles that were similar to those of blacks. They offered testimony about the need for bilingual election materials, threats of economic retaliation for participation, and polling locations being held in particularly hostile areas. With that in mind, Section 203 was incorporated into the VRA to require certain jurisdictions to provide written or oral language assistance in areas with high concentrations of citizens with limited English proficiency and illiteracy rates greater than the national average. In particular, the language assistance applied to four language minority groups: American Indians, Asian Americans, Alaskan Natives, and Latinos.

Nearly ten years passed between signage of the initial VRA, and the subsequent amendments formally recognizing non-black communities of color who were systematically excluded from the political process in various regions throughout the United States. The Amendments of 1975 were notable and far-reaching. Beyond merely extending the existing statutes, they broadened the scope of the bill, extending protections to include Hispanic voters and other ethnic groups whose primary language was not English. Further, the length of the extension was calculated with a primary purpose in mind: with an extension of seven years, the act would not expire until 1982, after the 1980 census and the consequent redistricting plans were to go into effect. Jurisdictions covered in 1965 would not be released until after they had effectively provided plans that were not in violation of Section 5.

This expansive action led to the steady growth of the number of minority voters and elected officials throughout the United States. It also paved the way for the growth of political and social organizations focused on increasing the visibility and success for communities of color more broadly. For the most part, however, the political gains of Latino groups vastly outnumber those made by Asian Americans and Native Americans.

AMENDMENTS AND CHALLENGES: 1980–1992

The 1980s played host to a number of major changes in voting rights that led to unprecedented gains in descriptive representation for racial minority groups at local, state, and federal levels. In the 1980 *City of Mobile v. Bolden* decision, the Supreme Court ruled that the proper standard in deciding Section 2 cases should be the ability to demonstrate purpose or intention to discriminate. Regarding Section 2 as a statutory restatement of the Fifteenth Amendment, it was held that the same judicial standard would be brought to bear on Section 2 cases. The majority decision upheld the use of at-large elections for the county commission seats in Mobile, Alabama, although no African Americans had been elected to the council since its inception in 1911. Without racially discriminatory intent, it was argued, neither Section 2 nor the Constitution prohibited electoral policies resulting in racially disparate outcomes.

As a reaction to the *Mobile* decision, Congress broadened the mandate of the VRA in 1982, both amending and extending the statutory provisions of the act. Prior to the 1982 amendments, Section 2 required that minorities demonstrate that the *intent* of a given redistricting procedure was discriminatory and would lead to minority vote dilution. Under the new version, any state procedure that had the *effect* of diluting minority vote strength was in violation and was subject to the review of the court system. Up to this point, it was incumbent upon states only to preserve the already existing minority districts, not to maximize that number (*Congressional Quarterly* 1993).

The 1982 Amendments made Section 2 permanent and extended specific sections, notably Sections 5, 6–9 (which allowed for federal examiners to monitor voter registration and election polls), and 203, for an additional twenty-five years. Perhaps the greatest divergence from prior civil rights laws was the results-based approach to electioneering. The effect of any given policy on the strength of minority participation, combined with any racially discriminatory effect that would effectively curtail minority representation in elected offices became the standard against which these policies would be compared.

Court cases repeatedly emerged, offering the Supreme Court the opportunity to clarify the meaning of the statutes. In *Thornburg v. Gingles* (1986), the Supreme Court endorsed the creation of minority districts wherever possible. At the same time that Congress had amended Section 2, the North Carolina General Assembly had adopted a new plan for state house and senate seats, including single and multi-member districts. In the *Gingles* case, African American voters contended that the plan, which included at-large countywide elections of state legislators, illegally diluted black voting strength.

The Supreme Court opinion delineated three conditions for Section 2 vote dilution violations to prevail:

1. The minority group must be able to demonstrate that it is sufficiently large and geographically compact to constitute a majority in a single-member district.

2. The minority group must be able to show that it is politically cohesive.

3. The minority must be able demonstrate that the white major- ity votes sufficiently as a block to enable it to defeat the minor- ity's preferred candidate.

Following the *Gingles* decision, the Department of Justice indicated that it would not preclear state redistricting maps that effectively di- luted minority vote strength. Prior to the case, it had required only that the states not provide retrogressive districting plans. External pressure on the states came from the Civil Rights Division of the Department of Justice for the creation of majority-minority districts. It was argued that the 1982 amendments to Section 2, combined with the *Gingles* ruling, required such districting to guard against minority vote dilution (Yarbrough 2002).

Thus, the redistricting plans following the 1990 census led to a number of historic breakthroughs: black candidates won House races in Alabama, Florida, North Carolina, South Carolina, and Virginia for the first time since the Reconstruction period, more than 100 years earlier. Illinois and New Jersey elected their first Hispanic representatives, and new Hispanic members increased the total numbers in California, Florida, New York, and Texas. The non-retrogression requirement of Section 5 ensured that all of the preexisting majority-minority districts stayed intact. Meanwhile, the new policy resulting from judicial opinions led to a newly inducted freshman class of 1993 including sixteen blacks and eight Latinos. This year marked the largest number of representatives from either group in the history of the federal legislature.

Most tellingly, this unprecedented wave of newly elected minority legislators set the stage for and provided the critical mass necessary to build a powerful, multiracial coalition. Though the experiences were not shared, per se, they were similar enough. Many came from communi- ties historically excluded from any form of meaningful participation, let alone leadership. Jim Clyburn (D-SC) became the first black president of the incoming freshman class of Representatives.

Minority political influence in Congress has fluctuated since the 1990s, often reflecting shifts in party control and acquired seniority. It has varied depending upon the ethnic group in question, it has also varied in relation to the shifting attitudes and political preferences of the larger, primarily white mainstream, and it has most certainly varied according to leadership (of all races and ethnicities, both internal and external to the political system) and with continually evolving opportunities for political mobilization.

The hard-fought challenges for minority gains in descriptive terms were precisely that: hard-fought. The lives lost and the risks at stake were many and high. A white supremacist racial order was state-sanctioned and manifested both in overt and covert forms. The entrenched racism in the United States was systemic and deep-rooted in both the political structures and the hearts of many Americans. That white supremacy was institutionalized as part of the development of the state, as well as the development of racialized political identities, has made minority gains in political influence complicated and exceedingly difficult. That vast numbers of Americans clung to (and in some cases, continue to cling to) extreme forms of prejudice further emphasizes the measure of resolve required to pursue avenues for political participation and descriptive representation.

Gains made during the Reconstruction period following the Civil War were quickly lost. For many people of color, they were never realized. It would not be until the 1960s that the United States government would make inroads to fulfill its promise, granting equal protection and the right to vote to citizens of color. The dynamic waves of increasing and decreasing influence vacillated with the varying prevalence of virulent racial orders, and the strength of coalitions built both within groups and among them.

Increases in descriptive representation arguably led to improved representation for racial and language minorities throughout the country. Representatives with more shared experiences with their constituents could and, in many cases, did lead to more thorough deliberation on issues that might otherwise have gone unnoticed. The growth of a more politically empowered community among racial and language

minorities has led to record levels of participation. Though successful achievement of policy preferences may remain limited, at the very
least, in the early twenty-first century, voices from various communities of color are present, they are accounted for, and other voices are
accountable to them.

Policy Influence in Influence Districts

You want to know why my civil rights support is lower than other
Democrats? Do you realize that every day in my district I'm called
a race traitor and an N-word lover???
                            —Member 12, White Southern Democrat (Influence District)

Does the legislative behavior of members of Congress reflect the types
of district they represent? Does the particular racial makeup of a district
affect their willingness to support civil rights legislation? Are there certain types of civil rights legislation that they are more willing to support
than others? What can we learn about the representation of influence districts, which were supported by the Supreme Court in 2003, and have
significant minority populations that nevertheless do not quite constitute
a majority? While some of these questions have already been addressed
by political scientists, an analysis of legislative behavior in light of the
Supreme Court's endorsement of influence districts seems both important and timely.

These questions present an implicit prelude to the rise of the
Congressional Tri-Caucus, and my theory of linked political fate, explored in Chapter 2. The backdrop of redistricting research, particularly
that referencing influence districts, follows a natural progression toward

both descriptive and substantive representation for racial minorities. If the strategy of creating influence districts yields few gains for legislators from and representing racial minority communities, the consequent approach—namely, to seek increased influence—occurs through multiracial coalitions.

The *Georgia v. Ashcroft* (2003) opinion set a precedent that allows state governments the legal wherewithal to significantly alter the distribution and allocation of minority citizens in legislative bodies at both state and federal levels. The Georgia State Legislature advocated the emphasis of influence districts—districts that have a 30–50 percent black voting age population—as a means to enhance black political influence at all levels. Citing specific political scientists along with notable members of the US Congress and the Georgia State Legislature, the Supreme Court ruled that

> In order to maximize the electoral success of a minority group, a State may choose to create number of "safe" districts, in which it is highly likely that minority voters will be able to elect the candidate of their choice. . . . Alternatively, a State may choose to create a greater number of districts in which it is likely—although perhaps not quite as likely as under the benchmark plan—that minority voters will be able to elect candidates of their choice. (16)

In so doing, the Court may have created a precedent under which states can opt to redistribute blacks and other racial minorities in such a way that would jeopardize their opportunities to achieve descriptive representation in legislative arenas. Though problematic in certain respects, the achievement of descriptive representation has been at the heart of the issue over racial redistricting for some civil rights advocates; other activists, however, decry the potential substantive policy losses for racial minority groups.

With influence districts in particular, there is a unique aspect to this study: How do we characterize their representation when compared to that of majority-minority districts and supermajority white districts?

In many ways, the representatives of influence districts are betwixt and between, and may be subject to more constraints while navigating the troubled waters of racial politics in the United States.

THE GEORGIA CASE

When the proposed Georgia redistricting plan was brought to the Federal District Court of Washington, DC for approval after the census was taken in 2000, preclearance was not granted. The question at hand concerned the distribution of predominantly minority communities throughout the multiple legislative districts, and whether the plan submitted by the state of Georgia was in accordance with Section 5 of the VRA of 1965. Was the new plan retrogressive? Would it compromise the electoral position of racial minorities in Georgia?

A number of elected Democrats from the General Assembly of Georgia, which includes the State Senate and State Assembly, along with a member of Georgia's congressional delegation, testified in front of the Supreme Court that they believed the new plan was not retrogressive. In fact, they argued, it would enhance the electoral position of minority voters in the state. The goal of the Democratic leadership of Georgia was to maintain the number of majority-minority districts, while simultaneously increasing the number of Democratic seats. They argued that they would be able to maintain the minority representation in the various legislative bodies, and that the increase in Democratic seats would lead to policies that benefited minorities throughout the state.

The Senate subcommittee that developed the plan at issue was vice-chaired by Senator Robert Brown, an African American who strongly supported the change in procedure. Congressional Representative John Lewis also supported the new redistricting strategy. Both believed that it was necessary to break up the heavily concentrated minority communities in order not to "waste votes."[1] It was also argued that blacks had a better chance to participate in the political process under a Democratic majority, so it was in the best interests of blacks to maximize the number of Democratic seats. Increasing the black voting age population above what was necessary to elect a Democratic representative, it was said, would "push the whole thing more towards [the] Republican[s]."[2] Senator Charles Walker, an African American, was the Majority Leader of the Georgia State Senate at the time. As he explained,

> In the past, you know, what we would end up doing was packing. You put all the blacks in one district and all whites in one district, so what you would end up with is [a] black Democratic district and [a] white Republican district. That's not a good strategy. That does not bring the people together. But if you put people together on voting precincts it brings people together.[3]

The plan passed through the Georgia General Assembly by a slight margin. Ten out of eleven black Senators favored the plan, and thirty-three of thirty-four black Representatives voted in favor of the new procedures. The Democratic Governor, Roy Barnes, signed it into law shortly thereafter. The new plan for the State Senate, which included fifty-six districts total, drew thirteen majority-minority districts, thirteen influence districts with a 30–50 percent black voting age population, and four districts with a 25–30 percent black voting age population.

In opposition to the new plan, the Office of the Attorney General at the United States Department of Justice submitted expert evidence of voting trends, highlighting racial polarization in specific areas. The Attorney General maintained that while a limited number of whites would support a black candidate, the percentage was insufficient "for black voters to elect their candidate of choice." Moreover, the districts were drawn by Democratic officeholders who enjoyed tremendous incumbent advantages when it came to their own reelections. Should those incumbents cease to run for office in that district, the likelihood of electing a Democrat, let alone an African American, substantially diminished, effectively limiting opportunities for both descriptive and substantive representation.

In the end, the five conservative Justices of the Rehnquist Court sided with the Democrats of Georgia. In a 5–4 vote, they opined that Georgia could follow through with its plan to maximize both majority-minority districts and influence districts. Citing the complexity that exists when trying to determine whether minority voters have the ability to elect a candidate of their choice, the Supreme Court set a precedent that loosened the burden on states that qualified as covered jurisdictions under the provisions of the VRA, stipulating that it would be acceptable for these states to create districts where it is feasible (albeit less likely than with the benchmark plan) for minority voters to elect candidates of their choice.

The Court further asserted that Section 5 of the VRA does not dictate the exact method of redistricting a state must employ. They argued that the influence minorities could exercise in a greater number of districts would serve the interests of the black community, and did not violate any non-retrogression requirements.

What happened in the election that followed was unexpected by Democrats and Republicans alike. The Democrats lost seats in both of the influence districts they had recently drawn, along with seats held by incumbents in majority-minority districts where the margin of advantage held by minorities decreased. The Senate transformed from a 30–26 Democratic majority, to a 30–26 Republican majority. Amid scandal, former Majority Leader Charles Walker, who ran for reelection in one of the new influence districts, lost his seat following enactment of the plan. Finally, an element of betrayal emerged: a number of white Democrats defected to the Republican Party, putting the Republican Party in firm control of committee chairmanships and all other leadership positions.

The congressional delegation experienced a very slight win. Democrats had projected a gain of four seats in the House. Prior to redistricting, there were eleven seats held by eight white Republicans and three black Democrats. Due to a sizable increase in population, Georgia gained two seats after the census count. The new lines left the Democrats expecting seven Democrats and six Republicans. In the elections immediately following the implementation of their redistricting plan, eight white Republicans, one white Democrat, and four black Democrats would serve in the US House of Representatives.

In both the State Senate and congressional plans, the Democratic pro-
jections were off considerably. Where did the plan go wrong? In Georgia,
the Democratic leadership was convinced that the new plan would work in
their favor, increasing their numbers while maintaining or increasing the
number of black elected officials. The plan did not work out the way they
expected. Though they gained seats (due in part to the increased number
of the overall delegation), the majority they expected in the congressional
delegation never came to pass. Even worse, amid scandal and betrayal,
they lost the control they once had to the Republican Party in the Senate.

The Georgia case is a prime example of the means not providing wherewithal for the end outcomes, which the Democratic legislators had in
mind. They argued for two immediate goals, which they believed would
lead to multiple desired outcomes. The first immediate goal they specified was 1) to increase black influence on electoral outcomes, which, they
argued, would lead to an increase in elected officials' responsiveness to the
interests and concerns of the black community and put into effect policies
that would benefit minorities throughout the state. The second immediate
goal was 2) to increase the number of Democratic representatives, which
would provide the opportunity to increase black participation in the political process as well, and again put into effect policies that would benefit
the statewide minority community. In all, they argued that maximizing
influence districts would increase black political power in the state.

Limited research has been conducted using empirical evidence to
analyze the political dynamics of representation for influence districts.
Does the existence of influence districts actually increase the influence
minorities can exert on policy initiatives? In current influence districts,
do we see representation that is noticeably different from other types of
districts? The answer to these questions depends heavily upon how we
define influence, and how we perceive influence in the electoral process
as a determinant of legislative behavior.

These questions fall into a greater framework of minority representation
in the United States, especially in the realm of legislative politics. How do minority groups, particularly ethnic minority groups such as blacks, Latinos,
and Asian Pacific Americans, gain political power and influence when their

lack of numbers places the needs of their communities at a disadvantage in the policy process? With a historically race-polarized electorate, the United States has had difficulty crafting a system that facilitates fair minority representation in the policy arena. What strategies will result in the best representation of the needs of marginal groups, given that the particular needs of these groups may not be directly relevant to the larger mainstream?

DISTRICT TYPOLOGY AND LEGISLATIVE BEHAVIOR

Following procedural changes in the early 1990s, wide-ranging research explored the policy of maximizing majority-minority districts in both state and federal legislatures, with mixed results. Theorists asked whether the specific focus on achieving descriptive representation for minorities through redistricting is at odds with the founding principles of the nation, and whether that descriptive representation would even produce the desired effect. Empirically, social scientists and legal scholars questioned whether majority-minority districts offer the best means for 1) achieving substantive representation for minorities, and 2) determining the ability of minorities to elect a representative of their choice. To date, most research has focused on either the policy consequences of majority-minority districts, or the achievement of descriptive representation for minority communities.

A 1996 analysis by Cameron, Epstein, and O'Halloran concludes that the best answer to redistricting in the South is to maximize the number of districts with slightly less than a majority of black voters. Outside the South, they prescribe the distribution of black voters equally among all districts (809). Additionally, they argue that the 65 percent rule enforced by the courts is more than is actually necessary to elect a minority representative; indeed, it dilutes minority voting strength.

Lublin (1999) counters the findings by Cameron et al., arguing that their lack of attention to the role of Latino voters led them to underestimate the importance of racial redistricting for the election of minority representatives. He argues that racial redistricting is indeed vital to the election of African Americans to the House, but that there is a potential tradeoff between descriptive and substantive representation, though that tradeoff exists in the South.

Canon (1999) came up with favorable findings concerning redistricting in the United States. Black majority districts, he argues, give blacks a greater voice in the political process. Black members of Congress do a better job of navigating racial issues and "balancing the distinctive needs of black voters and the general interests of all voters, black and white alike" (244). He contends that minority districting is a necessary component in achieving better substantive representation, and it works as a balancing biracialism, as opposed to a color-blind biracialism.

Furthermore, residence in a majority-minority district likely results in increased turnout among minority voters (Barreto et al. 2004). Exploring Latino voter patterns in Southern California over three general elections, Barreto, Segura, and Woods find that residence in a majority-minority district has a positive effect on minority voter turnout, and that the increased overlap of majority-minority districts (state assembly, state senate, and the House of Representatives) leads to increased likelihood that minorities will turn out to the polls on election day.

Switching the focus specifically to influence districts, Guinier (1994) laments the flaws inherent to the district model of representation broadly, and the use of influence districts in particular. The ability of minorities to successfully attain a degree of empowerment through a system that includes influence districts is questionable at best. Two distinct claims are made about influence districts: one argues that there is strong influence, the other that the influence is weak. The strong claim emphasizes that "the power of minority voters is superior because minority voters enjoy influence over multiple representatives rather than concentrated control over one or two." The claim of weak influence counters that "influence occurs only under the right combination of circumstances." The necessary circumstances for influence include the following:

- voting patterns in the geographic area are not racially polarized

- there are sufficient other racial groups to band together in support of a minority-sponsored candidate, if racially polarized voting is present
- there is significant fragmentation within the white community, if racially polarized voting is present.

Without any of these three circumstances, the weak claim stipulates that the ability for minorities to exert influence over an electoral outcome remains minimal. When racial polarization is present, "white officials are often unaware of black voters' decisive impact or deliberately ignore it because of even more decisive white support" (89).

Lublin's findings have multiple implications for influence districts. He finds that legislator responsiveness to black interests jumps significantly once a district reaches 40 percent black, which is considerably less than his estimated 50–55 percent black constituency required to elect an African American to office (1997, 72). He also argued that influence districts will only enhance the substantive representation of blacks under two conditions: first, that they have a black population of at least 40 percent, and second, that they do not result in the election of fewer Democrats (87).

Canon (1999) addresses both the history of blacks being elected in influence districts and the quality of representation for black citizens residing in influence districts. Only 35 of 6,667 elections in white majority House districts provided black winners from 1966 to 1996 (10). Out of those thirty-five elections, only one offered hope for the success of black candidates in white majority districts. He specifically cites the South, where the majority of black influence districts are found:

Given the patterns of racial bloc voting, no blacks were elected from majority white districts in the South in the 1980s or the 1990s. Two, Andrew Young (D-GA) in 1972 and Harold Ford (D-TN) in 1974, were elected in districts that were 44 percent black and 48 percent black, respectively, but both districts became majority black after the 1980 redistricting. (11–12)

In fact, most white representatives from black influence districts "do not spend much time representing their black constituents, while most black members of Congress spend a substantial portion of their time representing white constituents" (Canon 1999, 91). In an interview for this project, one member of the House of Representatives responded to that premise:

> The argument back then was 'White Democratic congressmen from influence districts don't really pay attention to the needs of minority voters, so we're not getting policies that we ought to get. At the very least what we should have are minority reps in congress and the state legislature and elsewhere that can then get these policies passed by developing the relationships, etc.' Seems to me that the best evidence of whether or not that's the case should be, if available, by an analysis of voting records . . ." (Member 12, White, South)[4]

That member's argument was predicated on the belief that the choice for the civil rights community in the South was to maximize majority-minority districts, which indirectly led to Republican control and thus no legislative success, or to opt for influence districts, which would allow for the Democrats to gain control, with a legislative success rate around 70 percent. What he did not address during the interview, despite multiple attempts to clarify, was the 30 percent of civil rights success that would not be achieved, and the implications of the high levels of racial polarization in the South. Moreover, he downplayed the potential benefits of descriptive representation.

Beyond anecdotes, the limited research available on influence districts does not seem to offer much more than highly conditional support for their ability to bolster the political efforts of racial minorities, both through substantive and descriptive forms of representation. To the contrary, significant evidence in the form of historical analysis as well as statistical evaluation, suggests that only under very specific conditions will minorities receive the quality of representation afforded them through the maximization of majority-minority districts, especially in the South.

DATA AND METHODS

I use tobit regression[5] to estimate the impact that specific variables have on member voting behavior (depending on the type of district the members represent) and their propensity to support civil rights policy. I create an index for each member, with the maximum cumulative total being 100, based on the level of support a member demonstrates for civil rights support (as defined by the Leadership Conference on Civil Rights[6]), then breaking that score down by the policy type: traditional civil rights or contemporary social welfare. Consequently, the membership of the House is evaluated for each category. Variables in the equation include the type of district (majority-minority, influence), socioeconomic information (educational attainment and median household income), regional location of the district (if the district is located in the South, and the percent of the district population that is urban), and personal characteristics of the legislators, including their racial backgrounds and partisan affiliations.[7]

Using data from the 2000 Unites States census, the Almanac of American Politics (2004, 2006), and the LCCR (Leadership Conference on Civil Rights) Voting Record for the 108th and 109th Congresses (2003–2004, 2005–2006), I analyze the relationship between legislative behavior toward different types of "civil rights" policy and the characteristics of the districts represented. Specifically with the census, I collected and calculated the voting age populations for all major ethnic groups, the percentage of the over-25 population that are high school graduates and college graduates; median incomes; percent of the population living below the poverty line; percent male and female by voting age; language ability; percent urban and rural; percent foreign born; type of district; and region of district. Using the Almanac of American Politics, I created variables for race, party, and gender for each Representative.

The use of LCCR scores has been challenged by some scholars for their questionable ability to accurately reflect the policy preferences of black constituents (Canon 1999). The goal of this statistical analysis is not necessarily to measure the specific desires of racial minorities, per se (these communities are anything but monolithic), but rather to try and gauge the amount of support provided for civil rights legislation by the legislators who represent them.

RESULTS

The focus of the tobit regression analysis hones in on the results from Tables 4.1 and 4.2, which directly address coalition districts for the 108th and 109th Congresses. Though comparisons can be made to the information on black majority/influence district models and Latino majority/influence models (provided in Appendix B for reference), the primary concentration is on the district's majority-minority status, and less on the specific minority group of the district.

It may go without saying that the most consistent, statistically significant variables were the partisan affiliation of the Representative, with Democrats offering much more support for civil rights across the spectrum, and whether the district was located in the Southern region of the United States. Starting with charismatic leaders like Hubert Humphrey, who equated civil rights to human rights at the 1948 Democratic Convention, the Democratic Party has consistently incorporated support for civil rights into the party platform for over sixty years.[8] Meanwhile, an overwhelming majority of white political leaders from the South have demonstrated continued, fervent resistance to the increased inclusion of racial minorities into virtually every aspect of economic and political decision-making processes, and have reliably opposed federal legislation that would promote racial equality both regionally and nationally. Though the size of this majority has decreased in recent years, and overt racist messages have been discouraged, support for measures that would promote racial equality, either through anti-discrimination policies or social welfare measures, have seen only limited success.

In both the 108th and the 109th Congresses, majority-minority district status is statistically significant when evaluating the voting behavior of representatives on traditional civil rights legislation. In the 109th Congress, there seems to be greater cohesion in the results. Representatives

Table 4.1 Tobit Estimates of the Effect of District/Legislator Characteristics on % Legislator Support for Civil Rights Legislation, Coalition Districts, 108th Congress

Independent Variable	LCCR Total Score	Traditional Civil Rights	Social Welfare
District Characteristics			
Black/Latino Majority	8.096	37.999**	4.202
	(5.247)	(14.115)	(5.557)
Black/Latino Influence	2.490	13.225	1.365
	(3.015)	(8.204)	(3.174)
South	−15.579***	−37.463***	−15.224***
	(2.002)	(5.893)	(2.111)
Income (deflated by $1000)	−.532***	−.706	−.561***
	(.144)	(.392)	(.153)
Education	60.895***	139.217**	62.089***
	(17.478)	(48.071)	(18.623)
Urban	16.598**	39.724*	10.720
	(6.320)	(17.266)	(6.665)
Representative Characteristics			
Democrat	75.017***	124.396***	75.034***
	(1.969)	(6.551)	(2.087)
Race (Black or Latino)	−4.323	−27.372*	.196
	(4.845)	(12.792)	(5.166)
Constant	14.356**	−44.463**	22.520**
	(4.957)	(14.180)	(5.229)
Number of Observations	434[a]	434	434
Pseudo R^2	.8694	.8234	.8619

NOTE: Numbers in parentheses are standard errors.

*p <. 05, **p < .01, ***p < .001.

[a] There are only 434 observations for the 108th Congress as a result of the transition between Bill Janklow (R-SD) and Stephanie Herseth (D-SD) that occurred midterm following Gov. Janklow's manslaughter conviction. This is a statewide at-large Congressional seat. Not only were there a number of missed votes for the district, but the party change and gender change of the representative made coding highly problematic, so the district was dropped.

Table 4.2 TOBIT ESTIMATES OF THE EFFECT OF DISTRICT/LEGISLATOR
CHARACTERISTICS ON % LEGISLATOR SUPPORT FOR CIVIL RIGHTS
LEGISLATION, COALITION DISTRICTS, 109TH CONGRESS

Independent Variable	LCCR Total Score	Traditional Civil Rights	Social Welfare
District Characteristics			
Black/Latino Majority	12.948*	14.941**	12.435
	(5.483)	(5.691)	(12.833)
Black/Latino Influence	.421	.582	.809
	(3.288)	(3.404)	(7.229)
South	−17.984***	−19.053***	−23.662***
	(2.175)	(2.257)	(4.668)
Income (deflated by $1000)	−.382*	−.395*	−.452
	(.159)	(.165)	(.325)
Education	62.356***	64.711***	89.222*
	(19.278)	(19.996)	(44.733)
Urban	16.907*	19.019**	13.946
	(6.855)	(7.106)	(14.985)
Representative Characteristics			
Democrat	70.624***	66.460***	111.232***
	(2.184)	(2.265)	(5.697)
Race (Black or Latino)	−2.514	−2.844	−.283
	(4.975)	(5.160)	(12.004)
Constant	14.302**	15.777**	9.009
	(5.353)	(5.550)	(11.435)
Number of Observations	435	435	435
Pseudo R^2	.8402	.8204	.7894

NOTE: Numbers in parentheses are standard errors.

*p < .05, **p < .01, ***p < .001.

from coalition majority districts show consistently strong support for civil rights legislation. Meanwhile, the corresponding support from legislators representing influence districts is less predictable. While on average there seems to be a mild, positive effect, the large standard errors suggest that the data is far from conclusive.

Increases in median household income in congressional districts appear to have a negative effect on a legislator's propensity to support more costly contemporary welfare issues for the 108th Congress, and shows a trend in both Congresses of increasing opposition towards all civil rights legislation as a constituency is more affluent, on average. This result contrasts, however, with greater numbers of college-educated individuals living within the district. In both Congresses, increased education (measured as an increase in the percentage of those aged 25 and older with college degrees) has a highly significant effect on support for civil rights legislation, in all three models: civil rights total, traditional civil rights legislation, and contemporary social welfare issues.

The percent of the population residing in an urban area also seems to increase the likelihood of support for civil rights, though to differing degrees and with varied levels of significance. This is generally consistent with my expectation that urban areas would have higher support, and may reflect a more cosmopolitan perspective on the need for racial equality.

On the whole, the directions of the coefficients for coalition districts were consistent with my expectations regarding support for civil rights legislation. While the significance varies depending upon the variable in question, there is sufficient data to point out trends and patterns in the roll call behavior.

DISCUSSION

Even with a somewhat small size dataset, Table 4.3 provides insight into the differing voting behaviors of members representing various types of districts. During the 108th Congress, there was a sizable difference in the

Table 4.3 MAJORITY DISTRICTS, INFLUENCE DISTRICTS AND SUPER-MAJORITY
WHITE DISTRICTS, 108TH AND 109TH CONGRESSES

Type of District	Average LCCR Score	Average Traditional Civil Rights Score	Average Social Welfare Score
Black Majority (21)	91.33	91.16	91.67
Black Influence (24)	68.21	63.10	71.18
Hispanic Majority (21)	78.71	79.59	78.18
Hispanic Influence (23)	76.44	76.40	76.45
Black/Hisp Majority (60)	86.43	85.95	86.81
Black/Hisp Influence (51)	59.77	57.70	60.95
White Supermajority (308)	37.23	32.84	39.72
Median	26.00	28.57	33.33
Mean	48.61	45.19	50.56

Supermajority white districts are districts with a white voting age population
greater than or equal to 70 percent, and a combined black and Hispanic voting age
population less than 30 percent.

legislative behavior of members representing districts with black/Latino
majorities and their corresponding influence districts. This dynamic is
important when considering the quality of representation being offered to
minorities both nationwide and at the local level. Though superficial, this
evidence suggests (as does more conventional knowledge) that the details
of district composition inform legislative behavior. For this research, the
behavior is limited to roll call support for civil rights legislation.

The data results provide substantive information about the voting patterns among different types of districts, even when controlling for the
partisan affiliation of the member of Congress. Much of the data suggests that there are indeed differing levels of support for civil rights when
we contrast the voting behavior of those representing majority-minority
districts, influence districts, and all other districts (mainly comprised of
white supermajorities), with the former providing the highest levels of
increased support.

Some of the electoral circumstances of the South may also affect the levels of support offered. Given that certain types of policies restricting the franchise are in much greater use in the Southern states (i.e., felon disenfranchisement laws), and that those policies more generally affect the racial minority populations of those states, members from the South may feel less compelled to support civil rights causes. That is, with higher levels of disenfranchised blacks and other minorities, representatives may be less inclined to protect their interests at the policy level, in that the electoral repercussions would be minimal.

An African American representative from the South was careful to highlight this dynamic during a research interview, offering that the voting age population percentages for each district may be misleading. He offered that there is substantial differentiation between the voting age population in his district, the percentage that is legally allowed to register to vote, the percentage that actually registers to vote, and then the "performance voters" that show up to the polls on election day. Though the drawing of district lines may be based on the voting age population, the people who make it to the polls do not necessarily reflect the district composition. His district, by definition, is a majority-minority district, but it is not the "safe" district that some of his colleagues in the Congressional Black Caucus represent.[9]

Another member offered the following regarding the potential changes to legislative redistricting that would emphasize influence districts:

> I believe that the redistricting policies that were put in place to create minority districts were absolutely necessary . . . And just like I support equal employment opportunity and affirmative action, I do not believe it's time to lay them aside. I am willing to consider influence districts, if I have no other options, if you tell me I can get influence districts and nothing else, then give me influence districts. (Member 11, Black, Midwest)

There are a few more important caveats to note. In both the 108th and 109th Congresses, at least one of the anti-discrimination policies that the LCCR took a stance on was related to sexual orientation discrimination. This fact, in and of itself, does complicate the analysis some. Neither black nor Latino communities are known for actively promoting tolerance along the lines of sexual orientation. Moreover, this fact may also help to explain part of the negative effect of district location in the South, where the salience of religious conservatism among various racial groups results in a higher percentage of persons rejecting gay rights in general and same-sex marriage in particular.

Similarly, there was an increase in perceived anti-Latino/anti-immigrant legislation during the 109th Congress. At least five measures cited by the LCCR dealt with harsh immigration policies, enhanced border issues, and the like. Though the Congressional Tri-Caucus generally did not support the legislation perceived to be targeting immigrants, and those of Latino descent in particular, many African American members did indicate in interviews that they felt pressure from their constituents to support extremely harsh immigration policies. One member cited the political commentator Lou Dobbs as one who was "irresponsibly fueling the flames" of anti-immigrant sentiment across the country.

Broadly speaking, advocates of civil rights at the federal level experienced tremendous hurdles in both the legislative and executive branches. The legislative constraints in the Republican-controlled House of Representatives during both the 108th and 109th Congresses are reflected every bit as much in the policy outcomes (where the LCCR had dismal success) as they are in the ability of representatives in the House to pose alternatives to legislation they deemed regressive (seldom were they allowed to offer amendments that would reduce the detrimental consequences of various measures to minority communities).

Though somewhat limited, the research presented here suggests that at the very least, members representing influence districts do not favor civil rights legislation in the same way or to the same degree as those representing majority-minority districts. In most cases, representation of an influence district suggests that members will be less likely to support anti-discrimination and social welfare policies than their majority-minority district counterparts, and only offer a minimal amount of support compared to those representing districts with white supermajorities. Moreover, what minimal support is actually offered by influence district representatives is not consistent enough to be relied upon. As such, one may be inclined to question whether the "significant influence" the Supreme Court stated would be in place is actually in effect, or if minority vote dilution is indirectly taking place in the policy process.

Power and Influence in the US House

Progressive Coalitions, Interracial Alliances, and Marginal Group Politics

Election is, of course, the all absorbing goal of every would-be House member. And reelection subsequently becomes the first order goal of almost every incumbent House member. But election is not the only goal that drives the aspirant towards politics in the first place, and reelection is not the only goal that keeps the member in politics afterwards. Nor, observably, is the electoral goal the crucial trace element in doping out each member's strategy of representation. Thus, while it is always necessary to recognize the first-order goal of most members is election or reelection, this single goal is rarely sufficient to explain their representational behavior.

—Fenno 2003, 6

Those who develop a sense of collective identity see that what they are experiencing is reflected in the conditions of the group of which they are a part. They are able to see that as a group they are dominated and exploited; they reject the legitimacy of their subordinate position, which they are able to understand as a

function of a system created by others; and they come to believe
that collective action is their best form of resistance.

—GUINIER AND TORRES 2002, 28

While considerable research has been conducted on the dynamics of
Congress—from the development and evolution of Congress as a political institution, to the sometimes unusual procedures employed in the legislative process—little attention has been paid to the means of garnering
and wielding influence for marginal groups. In a majority rule system
with finite resources, how do representatives from groups outside the
dominant mainstream navigate the political system and gain access to
resources in order to better meet their own specific needs?

The legislative representation of African Americans, Latinos, Asian
Pacific Americans, and other racial minority groups has also received considerable attention in recent years, due in large part to debates concerning
the substance of their representation, the increasing levels of inclusion
in the political process, and their relative ability to create policy change
that can benefit seemingly adverse political and economic circumstances.
With forty-three members in the Congressional Black Caucus, twenty-
three members in the Congressional Hispanic Caucus, and eleven members of the Congressional Asian Pacific American Caucus,[1] the absolute
numbers of racial minorities has increased in the Democratic Party, along
with their relative power. Even with the increases in influence for these
caucuses and their membership, various hurdles take center stage when
advocating for their constituents.

This chapter focuses on representative policy influence, that is, what
it means for legislators to have *real* political influence in the halls of the
Capitol. It both describes the circumstances of those members from and
representing sizable racial minority populations, and explains their representational strategies as they attempt to advocate for those communities. To
be sure, lawmakers have goals that extend far beyond reelection that affect
and shape their behavior in the institution. How do they achieve those goals?

How and when are coalitions formed? What has been the motivation to do so? How do members advocating for groups that have been historically ex- cluded from politics advance an agenda that is more progressive than the status quo? Conversely, must they also guard the status quo from conserva- tive actions that would worsen the situation of their minority constituents?

In part, this chapter offers an insider's look at the struggles of mem- bers of Congress from and representing marginalized groups across the country, racial minorities in particular. After 1990, with vast changes in redistricting policies, a much more diverse legislative branch was born. In so doing, more and more minorities were elected and consequently granted the opportunity to operate *inside* the margins—becoming a very part of one of the dominant structures from which they had historically been excluded. As such, I also explore internal hurdles in a system that largely favors both a status quo and those social groups who have already reaped the benefits of privilege and inclusion.

To conduct this research, I collected new data through interviewing forty-seven Members of Congress (sometimes referred to as MCs). I paid considerable attention to racial group identity, district type, whether the legislator was from the South, and other background factors that poten- tially impacted personal attitudes and consequent legislative behavior af- fecting marginal groups. These interviews were semi-structured, which offered the opportunity for follow-up questions when appropriate, and were tailored to the member based upon her voting record.

Using this data, I find that while members from and representing marginal groups have varying histories, those who perceive a personal link to racial or ethnic injustice seem much more willing to denounce such practices and to remedy these situations through a variety of means. There was also widespread (though not universal) belief among Democrats of black, Latino, and white descent that the political fates of blacks and Latinos were strongly linked to each other. Among black and Latino members, considerable anecdotal evidence suggested that the structural hurdles to gaining political influence were much higher for them than for their white counterparts, and that subtle prejudice frequently occurred in the House of Representatives, due in part to their racial background and in part to the demographics of the districts they were elected to represent.

GROUP INTERESTS, INTERGROUP RELATIONS, AND POLITICAL RACE

A broad array of dynamics surfaces when addressing group representation, regardless of the group being represented. The nature of substantive representation, as explored by Pitkin, can have two interpretations, which are compatible at times and inconsistent at others. In many instances the pivotal question is not whether constituents are being substantively represented, but whether that representation is extrapolated vis à vis their perceived *interests*, or if it is understood vis a vis their perceived *preferences*. In specific cases, an elected official may equate these two (interests and preferences) as the same, but in various instances, the official may view the two as entirely different and/or mutually exclusive. To stand up for, or protect, a certain group does not necessitate behavior that reflects the group's preferences, if the enactment of said preferences is likely to result in harm to the group as a collective.[2]

Applied to marginalized communities and interracial interactions, group politics and representation is often categorized in one of three ways: cooperation, competition, or a combination thereof (McClain 2006). In each case, however, there is no definite answer to a group's actual best interests. With finite resources that a municipal, state, or federal government can provide, groups often compete over resource distribution and such tangibles as jobs, healthcare, and housing. Historically, political alliances have been drawn along the lines of race, with policy decisions over finite resources often framed (and in many cases, rightfully so) as a zero-sum game. Hero and Preuhs take this approach a bit further—competition and cooperation, they argue, are two of four dynamics taking place in black-Latino relations at the national level, also including independence and negotiation. Their analysis concludes that black and Latino MCs largely act independently of one another (2013).

Kauffman has conducted considerable research on interracial interactions at the local level, racialized mass attitudes, and the propensity
of blacks and Latinos to build electoral coalitions. Based upon a premise that perceived commonality between blacks and Latinos is integral
to constructing political association, Kauffman examines factors corresponding to cross-racial affinities and participation in minority-oriented
political alliances (2003, 199). Finding that pan-Latino affinity is a prominent indicator of Latino-black commonality, her work suggests that those
Latinos with a strong sense of ethnic pride may actually better identify
with African Americans. She also finds, in turn, that long-term political
acculturation is unlikely to result in particularly high levels of closeness to
blacks. Finally, the role of leadership is discussed, with particular attention
paid to Latino leadership, to determine whether Latinos will become more
unified as a group and more inclusive of other minority groups (208).[3]

What prescriptions have been offered regarding coalition-building
among marginal communities, particularly among racial minorities?
Guinier and Torres (2002) explore an idea of "political race" that focuses
more heavily on the bonds shared by those trying to eradicate racial injustice as it manifests in numerous forms. Their normative claims navigate the complex environment of race, rejecting the notion that the sole
determinant of race is skin color, and offering the premise that action
and commitment, rather than predetermined descriptors, would guide a
more politicized understanding of race-consciousness (13–14).

> For a progressive cross-racial coalition to emerge, whites need to
> engage with race, and blacks need to engage with a more inclusive
> vision of social justice. Both types of engagement require a different
> understanding of the meaning of race and its relationships to
> power. (31)

Applied to legislative behavior, multiple implications surface here. First,
a broad definition of civil rights must be adopted by representatives of
and advocates for marginal groups in order to eradicate systemic injustice. Second, racism and other structural power dynamics must be actively

engaged with, rather than dismissed as unimportant or irrelevant by those elected by more dominant or mainstream constituencies. Finally, the marginalized experiences that occur both in the House of Representatives as well as back home in their constituencies must be acknowledged and understood by legislators as they create policy, given that they are in the position to promote equality and fairness in government.

All of these implications require a deeper understanding of the precedence of power and oppression in the United States—both on the part of legislators and American culture at large. Group politics in this country has long historical roots and contemporary manifestations that emerge throughout multiple stages of the legislative process. There are complex dynamics of power and dominance at play when contemplating the history of exclusion in the political process—most (if not all) of which have never been rectified, let alone acknowledged. Moreover, progressive movements toward equality by marginal groups have often been met with brutal hostility and flagrant contempt by those in power, further compounded by the apathy of a larger mainstream.

SUBTLE PREJUDICE AND INTERSECTIONAL MARGINALIZATION

Subtle prejudice takes on a variety of forms including, but not limited to, unequal treatment, information-withholding, dismissal of grievances and requests, and other behaviors based consciously or subconsciously upon negative racial stereotypes. Ayres, who studies various forms of discrimination in retail markets, holds that there is a widespread implicit belief among Caucasian males that race and gender discrimination are not serious problems that merit scrutiny. His research concludes that these types of discrimination are, in fact, pervasive, and subsequently detrimental to those subject to them, while a large portion of the dominant group remains ignorant of their experience (2001).

Evidence also suggests that not all groups are treated with similar regard in Washington, or rather, that not all groups are advocated for equally in American politics. Strolovitch (2006) finds that advocacy organizations are considerably less active when it comes to issues affecting disadvantaged subgroups of the US populace than they are when advocating for their more advantaged counterparts. In turn, this dynamic serves as a reinforcing tool where certain subgroups, particularly those with two or more of the following signifiers—racial minorities, women, LGBT, and the poor—are continually marginalized and their needs are more likely to be dismissed and/or misrepresented as narrow and particularistic. That is, individuals who suffer from intersectional marginalization—multiple forms of discrimination such as racism, sexism, classism, homophobia, and the like—are often poorly represented by interest groups that only advocate for racial equality, gender equality, and other forms of single-axis consensus issues.

LINKED POLITICAL FATE AND MULTIRACIAL COALITION-BUILDING IN THE HOUSE

Throughout history, even during periods of tremendous change, the status quo in legislative procedure and privilege has been largely accommodated, and only wide-ranging coalitions have served as catalysts for change to occur. Even so, coalitions seeking reform often build new rules over long-standing foundations of privilege, meaning that real change, though possible, can be painfully slow in the making (Schickler 2001). While singular interests remain insufficient to generate major change, intersections of various groups are much more effective at driving change in Congress.

Often due to shared experiences and histories, members within various racial groups (particularly African Americans) perceive a linked fate that is shared with others who have like characteristics (Dawson 1994). This dynamic, Dawson argues, serves as one explanatory factor in black voting behavior: namely, that black voters are more likely to vote for a party that is perceived to best serve the group interests because their individual fate is inextricably tied to the fate of the group. Black voting patterns, though perplexing to some scholars, tend to be quite logical. Throughout American history, the life chances of individual blacks have been largely tied to group status, and their political involvement reflects this dynamic.

> The central assumption . . . is that the more one believes one's own life chances are linked to those of blacks as a group, the more one will consider racial group interests in evaluating alternative political choices. (Dawson 1994, 75)

In macro-level politics, where representatives are from and representing various marginal groups including but not limited to racial minorities, I argue that linked fate occurs on a more grandiose scale. That is, when these representatives arrive in Washington, they realize that the fate of their constituencies depends solely upon their ability to forge coalitions and accrue enough support to successfully advocate an agenda that includes their constituents, rather than allow the status quo to continue down the path of marginalization. The fate of their constituents cannot (and arguably should not) rest solely upon racial solidarity. Instead, the fates of their constituents often rest with the fates of other similarly marginalized groups, despite their varying histories and cultural distinctions. Thus, their experiences can be categorized as a *linked political fate*, where although these groups do not share the same cultural history, their representatives realize that their fates are particularly linked to the fates of groups similarly stigmatized and excluded by a larger mainstream.

From an initial standpoint, this begs the question of whether the potential coalitions built between minority groups are more the result of an "enemy of my enemy is my friend" perspective than that of a perceived linked political fate among representatives of marginalized communities. This common enemies concept is a recurring trend in coalition-building, both domestically and globally. That said, understanding marginal group politics in the United States House of Representatives requires careful attention to relationships of power in terms of history, one's constituency, the demographic makeup of the body of Congress, as well as the structural foundations and rules that constrain the lawmaking process.

The distinct differences between a common enemies perspective and that of my linked political fate theory are as follows: first, there is the unique position of marginalization. My theory of linked political fate requires that the groups working together suffer currently from societal stigmatization and limited inclusion among economic and political elites. Second, they have been historically excluded from elites based upon their marginal group status, and the duration of their exclusion lasted for multiple generations. Finally, in terms of legislative behavior, the entire legislative body has been unwilling or unable to pass reforms that would effectively eliminate or significantly reduce their continued levels of stigmatization and deprivation. That is, the persistence of exclusion manifests through the inability to have fluctuating coalitions that would allow marginal groups to succeed in passing legislation, which would prevent the perpetuation of the inequality and discrimination they face.

As such, a common enemies perspective is much too broad to capture the particular dynamics of linked political fate, because it does not allow for the current and historical context of marginalization. Further, it does not allow one to consider the structure of an institution itself as inherent to the obstacles that marginal groups face. With the passing over generations, the marginalization becomes systemic, and is not merely the direct result of individual actors and isolated events.

Whether cooperation, competition, independence, or negotiation occurs at the grassroots level of politics back home in their districts, representatives at the "grass tops" level deal in a different landscape, fighting over a much larger and more comprehensive pie. To gain influence in the policy process, they engage in fundraising activities (for their reelection campaigns, the reelection campaigns of their colleagues, party dues, and party-designated swing district races), vie for important committee posts, and work to gain positions in leadership where they can better influence the party apparatus.

I ask whether there is a *collective intersectional marginalization* that occurs in the legislative process, not only based on the characteristics of a given representative, but also on the demographics of the district he or she represents. That is, with geographic concentrations of race and poverty in various districts, those representing such districts and their constituents experience multiple manifestations of marginalization, including dismissal, exclusion, and stigmatization.

This, of course, has drastic consequences for these groups, who have been systematically excluded from government and policy outcomes in the past. Not only have they been underrepresented and underserved throughout American history (that much should not be subject to debate), but their current marginal status continues, through various subtle means, to determine policy outcomes, and consequently their hopes for the future. There is an often unspoken irony in the American political process: by nature of the institutions in place, those communities in greatest need of assistance are the least likely to be able to obtain it.

My overarching premise is as follows: bolstered by increased numbers following the elections of 1992, and in response to high levels of marginalization under Republican control of the House from 1995 to 2006, lawmakers from and representing racial minority groups built and sustained an alliance based upon a perceived linked political fate. In part, forged as a strategy to amass numbers and gain influence in the majority rule, winner-take-all aspect of congressional politics, over time this alliance solidified and gained strength, resulting in a unique coalition with the potential to create substantive change that could directly benefit the marginalized communities they represent, and indirectly extend those benefits to other marginal groups.

The initial formalization of this robust coalition took place in April 2002, when lawmakers from and representing racial minorities convened a summit in Leesburg, Virginia, providing the foundation that would later become the Congressional Tri-Caucus, an umbrella group comprised of all members from the Congressional Black, Hispanic, and Asian Pacific American Caucuses. In most cases, their agenda extends beyond advocacy for racial equality, and includes the denunciation of multiple manifestations of discrimination experienced by a broader collection of marginal groups, including, but not limited to, women, lesbians and gays, and the poor. Moreover, their agendas include substantive social policy issues that would benefit this broad collection of groups.

METHODS

To better explore these ideas, I sought personal interviews with members
of the House of Representatives, to find out about their experiences and
observations. I contacted each Capitol office of the members of the House
of Representatives requesting confidential, in-person, thirty- to sixty-
minute interviews, depending upon the amount of time they could afford
me. I interviewed almost fifty members of the House of Representatives
and inquired about their representation techniques, their views on the
future of interracial alliances, and how they defined influence in the political process. Further, I inquired about the demographics of their district, and whether they felt the racial breakdown of their district affected
their policy decisions. Finally, I asked whether they believed a linked political fate existed between blacks, Latinos, and other marginal groups,
and how much, if at all, they believed that racial dynamics internal to the
House played a role in policy outcomes.

This sample of the House of Representatives was not random. Inevitably,
an issue of response bias arose in this process. Members of Congress who
already demonstrated a greater interest in civil rights and voting rights
seemed much more willing to participate in a confidential interview on
the topic. Similarly, former academics now serving in Congress seemed
much more willing to sit down and chat with an aspiring academic.
Members of the Congressional Black and Hispanic Caucuses participated
in disproportionate numbers, as did members of the Democratic Caucus.
During the summer of 2006, one Republican member indicated that the
Democrats had much more free time in order to participate.[4]

Perhaps more importantly, these interviews were subject to any number
of constraints, the most prominent being time. Some interviews had to be
stopped or postponed because the members were called into votes, into
confidential leadership meetings, and unexpected caucus meetings. As a
result, while most questions were uniformly asked, some questions were left
unanswered due to time constraints. Interviews ranged from twenty-five
minutes to nearly two hours in duration. Inevitably, some members were
more talkative than others, and some had a greater penchant for digression.

All interviews were conducted between June 2006 and January 2008. This timeframe also produced some unique dynamics, the most prominent being the majority party change that occurred after the November 2006 elections, which put the Democrats in control of the House for the first time in twelve years. This switch also resulted in significant gains for those members representing racial minorities and other marginal groups. With the partisan shift, so too arose a more dramatic shift in the ability for those from and representing marginal groups to have a pronounced effect on agenda-setting in the House of Representatives, which was readily apparent in the responses given during interviews.

PARTICIPANT INFORMATION

In total, forty-seven Members of the House of Representatives participated in this survey. An additional eight members agreed to interview, but time constraints served as a hurdle. Of the participants, twenty-one are Caucasian, seventeen are African-American, and nine are Latino. Two of the aforementioned members also served on the Executive Board of the Congressional Asian Pacific American Caucus. There were multiple ways that one might be concerned over response bias: only seven women participated,[5] and only seven Republicans took part. All participants held office during the 109th Congress, though many were interviewed during the first year of the 110th Congress. No delegates or resident commissioners participated.

A balanced cross-section of senior and junior legislators participated in this survey. The average number of years a participant served as a Representative in the House was ten years, with twenty-five of the participants having served ten years or longer, and fourteen members serving their first or second terms during the 109th Congress.

The types of district represented also spanned a broad spectrum in terms of racial demographics: there were fourteen districts with a supermajority white population, nine districts with a black majority, seven districts with a Latino majority, seven districts with a black/Latino combined majority, four districts with a black influence population, two districts with a Latino influence population, three districts with a black/ Latino combined influence population, and one plurality-majority district, where the combined Asian/black/Latino population totaled more than 50 percent.[6]

While the most recent figures for national poverty indicate that 12.3 percent of the public is living at or below the poverty rate,[7] there are distinct differences among my participants. The average poverty rate for those interviewing was 17.57 percent. Broken down by district type and race of the representative provides much more telling information, as can be seen in Tables 5.1 and 5.2.

Given the dramatic differences in poverty rates when compared with both the racial composition of the district, as well as the racial background of the Representative in the House, there are overlapping issues that extend beyond race to poverty, or beyond poverty to race. That there are higher concentrations of poverty in communities of color should not be surprising,[8] but this information provides some insight into the

Table 5.1 POVERTY RATES BY RACE OF REPRESENTATIVE (109TH CONGRESS)

District Poverty Rate by Race of Representative	Representative White	Representative Black	Representative Latino	Average Total
Interview Participant	12.25	20.97	22.80	17.57
Entire Chamber	10.95	20.07	22.33	12.37

Table 5.2 POVERTY RATES BY DISTRICT TYPE

District Poverty Rate by District Type	Majority-Minority	Influence	Supermajority White	Average
Interview Participant	21.69	16.73	10.51	17.57
Entire Chamber	21.74	15.66	10.17	12.37

participating interviewees, in terms of who they represent. For many of the lawmakers from and representing communities of color, their districts also disproportionately house America's poor.

PATTERNS IN RESPONSES

A number of patterns emerged throughout the course of the interviews, which I will outline here, then explain in detail further on. First, nearly all interviewees, regardless of race, identified a linked political fate between blacks and Latinos, and with other marginal groups to a lesser extent. Representatives from and representing these groups (and serving as members of the CBC, CHC, or CAPAC) indicated a very high rate of support for the other groups comprising the Tri-Caucus. In many cases, these members pointed to polarizing issues such as gay marriage and immigration as unpopular back home in the district. Nonetheless, most had voted against the gay marriage amendment banning marital status for same-sex couples, and against legislation to build a fence along the US–Mexico border. A psychological proximity to discrimination or injustice seemed to heighten all members' awareness of, and consequent support for, civil rights legislation.[9] Frequent instances of subtle racism were detailed by black and Latino members as they explained their representational strategies and experiences as lawmakers. Finally, there was strong support for the idea that district type influenced policy outcomes, where the concentrations of poor minorities led to additional forms of subtle racism and exclusion in the legislative process.

LINKED FATE AND MARGINAL COALITIONS

Respondents voiced very strong beliefs that the political fortunes of blacks and Latinos were linked, though a few added caveats about how long this would last, given the relative growth of the Latino community. Thirty-eight of the forty-seven interviewees thought there was a linked political fate between those two groups in particular. Of the nine respondents who were unsure or believed that there was no linked fate, six were Republican.[10]

> Latinos and blacks definitely have linked fates. The problem is the people aren't in sync with the leaders. Even educated black people don't like Latinos. What we're doing isn't working. The only way to change the system is through coalitions. (Member 15, Black, Mid-Atlantic)

> I'm not sure if they have linked political fates, I think that's what you called it. But I assure you, if the Republicans are going after [Latinos] now, they're coming after us next! (Member 22, Black, South)

> Latino immigration should not be a wedge issue. We need to combine our resources to fight for more. We can't afford to get fooled by the fraud they're trying to perpetuate between our communities. (Member 2, Black, Midwest)

Most of the respondents indicated that they occasionally voted and behaved contrary to the preferences of their constituents when they felt the issue was not salient, or when they believed that constituent preferences ran counter to the needs of the entire district. They offered that there were multiple issues on which their constituents had strongly negative or positive feelings, but their own sentiments were not passionate. A few pointed out that their constituents (like many Americans) took little interest in any legislation on the Hill, which meant that a significant percentage of their voting behavior did not weigh heavily on their reelection concerns. As such, they relied solely upon their own judgment in instances where their constituents held no position on the issue.

The difficulty, one member noted, was that discriminatory measures often reached the national stage, particularly measures that were directed against the LGBT and Latino communities. She stated that if she felt a piece of legislation was discriminatory and/or acted against the interests of her constituents, she would not support it, even if that meant overlooking the preferences of her constituents. These instances often included more polarizing issues such as gay marriage and immigration. The problem, she noted, was that there were any number of pieces of legislation that the Republicans had passed on the Hill that had a direct negative impact on her constituents and particularly on the poor, women, and communities of color that went completely unaddressed by the media. The polarizing issues that received disproportionate amounts of media attention, it seemed, directly targeted specific marginal groups, but that was where awareness ended. The debate was often manipulated through the exploitation of certain cleavages, inciting negative feelings among the public that inhibited the formation of policy for the common good. Nobody back home was interested in, let alone willing to mobilize against, bankruptcy reform, tax cuts for the wealthy, and other pet projects offered by the Republican members of Congress.

> The churches in my district are not happy about gay marriage. They don't like it. It's my job to help move my African American constituents to a different level relative to that issue. I try to explain it as human rights, which includes immigration, gay rights, and civil rights. (Member 2)

Nineteen members cited the gay marriage ban as discriminatory, and that any allowances for discriminatory policy would hurt racial minorities as a group. All but one Latino interviewed opposed harsh immigration measures, and believed that it was very discriminatory toward them. Of the black and white respondents, an additional seventeen volunteered that they opposed harsh immigration measures, though many acknowledged that their constituents had developed negative attitudes toward Latino immigrants, often related to a lack of good jobs available in their communities.

Coalitions were definitely a primary concern among members of the Congressional Tri-Caucus.

> In order for [blacks and Latinos] to have a unified effect on public policy, there has to be a common strategy and unified support.

For us—healthcare, education, the economy—it's more important. It's life or death. We have to be conscious of efforts to divide and conquer. (Member 14, Latino, Southwest)

Many of the members of the Congressional Black Caucus saw support for the Latino community as paramount to the cause of fighting injustice. They argued that

Civil rights isn't a principle when you're fighting for yourself. That's called general self-interest. It's when you're willing to walk for someone else that it means something [chuckling]. (Member 5, Black, South)

A number of caveats rise in relation to black and Latino alliances in the United States that should not be ignored within any assessment. They include (but are not limited to): national origin, and region of current residence. Explained in greater detail in earlier chapters and in other scholarly research, variations in interracial relations can play a crucial role in the cooperative process of coalition-building. For instance, in New York City, where black and Latino communities have overlapped for years, and where that overlap started generations earlier in Puerto Rico and other locations within the Caribbean, we find Representatives that have built long-term alliances and friendships. Coalition-building has been much more strained in the Southwest, where the Latino population is the fastest-growing demographic group, but is more often portrayed as immigrants and "outsiders."

On average, there seemed to be a strong working relationship between the members of the Congressional Black and Hispanic Caucuses, who were eager to report that the Congressional Asian Pacific American Caucus was also an equal contributor to the newfound coalition. Channels of communication remained open, largely coordinated by the executive directors of each caucus. Members of both groups excitedly illustrated the inroads that had been made over the past five years, and were optimistic about future alliances that would allow them to better meet the needs of their constituents.

CIVIL RIGHTS LEGISLATION IN THE 109TH CONGRESS

A number of very different pieces of legislation were introduced during the 109th Congress, representing the broad spectrum of civil rights issues before the House of Representatives, which can be used for comparison when considering the responses offered by participants. Among them were the Fannie Lou Hamer, Rosa Parks and Coretta Scott King Voting Rights Act Reauthorization and Amendments Act (H.R. 9), the Secure Fence Act of 2006 (H.R. 6061), and a constitutional amendment proposal banning same-sex marriage and prohibiting the government from recognizing same-sex marriages sanctioned in certain states (H.J. Res. 88). I specifically selected these three pieces of legislation because they provided straightforward voting behavior on a traditional civil rights issue, an issue directly focused on Latino immigrants, as well as one focused toward members of the LGBT community.[11]

Reauthorization of the VRA, despite four exceedingly controversial amendments from the Republican Party, was fairly straightforward. On final floor passage, the bill received 390 votes, with thirty-three opposed, and nine not voting. All members of the Congressional Asian Pacific American, Black, and Hispanic Caucuses voted in favor of this piece of civil rights legislation. Of the three caucuses, fifty-seven members served as cosponsors of the bill. Of my participating interviewees, all voted in favor of the bill, and thirty-one served as cosponsors.

The Secure Fence Act of 2006 provides a more telling scenario of coalition work between the racial minority caucuses. Introduced by Rep. Peter King of New York, H.R. 6061 had forty-two cosponsors, and considerable support along both sides of the aisle, passing with 283 votes in favor, and 138 votes against.[12] The bill included multiple components, the most prominent being the direction of the Homeland Security Secretary to construct at least two layers of reinforced fencing along the United States–Mexico border, along with the installation of additional physical barriers, in order to gain operational control of US-international land borders.

Despite demonstrable bipartisan support, there were no cosponsors of H.R. 6061 in the Tri-Caucus, and only six members voted in favor of the legislation, with Rep. Cleaver (D-MO) not voting.[13] Moreover, three of the five Republican members of the Congressional Hispanic Conference (a separate entity from the Hispanic Caucus) broke with their party and voted against the bill. Of my interviewees, only one served as a cosponsor of the legislation, while an additional fourteen voted in favor of the bill.

Finally, three joint resolutions prohibiting gay marriage were brought up in the House of Representatives during the 109th Congress: the first was sponsored by Rep. Dan Lundgren of California (H.J. Res. 39); the second was sponsored by Rep. Marilyn Musgrave of Colorado (H.J. Res 88); and the final resolution was sponsored by Rep. Louis Gohmert of Texas (H.J. Res. 91). Of the three constitutional amendments proposed, only H.J. Res 88 made it to the floor, while the remaining two stalled in the Judiciary Committee. Musgrave's proposed amendment had 134 cosponsors, and received 236 votes on the floor.

Support for gay rights among racial minority legislators seems slightly weaker in this case than it did for the fence legislation, particularly when contrasted with their white counterparts in the Democratic Party. The proposed amendment received thirty-four Democratic votes over-all. Of the Congressional Black, Hispanic, and Asian Pacific American Caucuses, eight members voted in favor of the legislation, and only one— Rep. Sanford Bishop (D-GA)—served as a cosponsor.[14] Three members— Rep. Danny Davis (D-IL), Rep. Ruben Hinojosa (D-TX), and Rep. Cynthia McKinney (D-GA)—went on the record as "not voting." Of my interview-ees, seven served as cosponsors of H.J. Res 88, while ten voted for it on the floor. Another three went on record as "not voting." Requiring a two-thirds majority as a constitutional amendment, which it did not receive, the measure failed.

One of my interviewees, a member of the Black Caucus who voted in favor of the constitutional ban on gay marriage, referred to that specific vote as an instance where he had to "hold his nose." In his district down South, he argued, he was expected to vote against gay marriage, no matter what his personal preferences were. He had to pick his battles, and for him that meant picking between supporting his Latino colleagues on im-migration issues or supporting gay marriage. He opted for immigration because his district was more amenable to Latinos than to homosexuals, though his district lacked support for both (Member 7, Black, South).

Multiple black members from the South voiced similar concerns related to their constituent preferences. Should they stray too far from their more conservative voters (many of whom were more conservative on "religious" issues, and obtained the bulk of their political information through religious networks), they would effectively invite a primary challenge. They cited the media fanfare around specific issues that would result in increased news ratings and profits, but simultaneously result in additional pressure on legislators to reflect public opinion in their voting behavior, and that opinion was frequently at odds with optimal policy solutions.

PERSONAL EXPERIENCE AND BACKGROUND

More than three-quarters of the participants pointed to their personal backgrounds as a source for their high levels of support for civil rights. In repeated instances they demonstrated their personal attachment to injustice and discrimination as the centerpoint of their decision to advocate for civil rights. For instance, each of the three Jewish members interviewed had a 100-percent support rating, according to the Leadership Conference on Civil Rights. In each case, they noted the historical ties between Jewish leaders and black leaders in the 1960s, and how when they were growing up, they were taught that racial and ethnic discrimination had to be curtailed.

> My parents taught me that there was a strict prohibition on treating people differently on the basis of race. Growing up in the Jewish community, which had experienced horrible discrimination in the past, I felt I understood the sting of racial marks. Even though the nature of the prejudice was different, and people couldn't necessarily see my religion, there's an empathy that comes from that experience. (Member 32, White, Pacific)

There are some people who talk about having friends who are minorities, but they don't actually talk about race. I have black friends *and* I believe what they tell me. (Member 3, White, Mid-Atlantic)

I remember being a little kid and seeing a sign that read "No dogs or Mexicans allowed." People get separated early on into certain communities, jobs, and stations in life. (Member 31, Latino, Pacific)

SUBTLE RACISM

It'd be nice if they learned how to say my name.

—Member 31, Latino, Pacific

In many instances, lawmakers from the Congressional Black and Hispanic Caucuses relayed experiences of subtle racism and preconceived ideas their professional acquaintances held that left them feeling slighted and annoyed. At times, these slights were minimal, but in other cases, they had sizable consequences.

I don't think we're entirely shut out, but in some instances, we're completely invisible. Opinions of African Americans may not be valued as much as our white counterparts. There are some African Americans who have gained more power, but it's at the cost of suppressing their true feelings. (Member 15)

You feel the discrimination. You feel like you are being under-estimated and undervalued. There's a constant struggle to be heard and you have to fight the undervaluing and the underestimation. What's worse, because you represent a certain constituency, your opinion doesn't carry weight. (Member 14)

Most of the members who identified as racial minorities could point to various slights that they or their colleagues had experienced during their tenure in the House. In some cases, the emotional response appeared to be resentment, though in others it was simple disappointment tempered by resignation. One African American male relayed a story of his close friend in the House (another African American male) being stereotyped as a convicted felon. He offered that racism in this country was so pervasive, that no matter how hard one might work, negative prejudices remained an inevitable reality.

One widespread complaint emerged regarding intelligence. Many of the black and Latino members disliked the seemingly condescending treatment they received[15], particularly when they voiced opposition to specific legislation or amendments. The issue was not that they misunderstood the bill; rather, they simply disliked the proposed law, believing it to be bad policy. When they would clarify their point, so as to assert their understanding of the complex issue, they would be summarily dismissed.

DISTRICT MARGINALIZATION

District-level marginalization was also a trend in member responses. One member admitted that, at times, he felt demoralized when trying to explain to his colleagues in committee that his constituents were just as important as theirs (Member 28, Black, South).

On multiple occasions, lawmakers from and representing districts with large minority populations and high poverty rates expressed discontent with the Democratic Party apparatus, and with then-DCCC Chair Rahm Emanuel (D-IL) in particular.[16] In multiple ways, money is infused into every aspect of the political side of legislative politics. In order to gain status within the Democratic Party, each member must pay considerable dues, gained through fundraising. In the 109th Congress, dues ranged from $600,000 in the case of the Minority Leader, to $125,000 for the rank and file members. Those members in leadership were expected to contribute at least $400,000, while those serving as exclusive committee ranking members ($300,000), exclusive subcommittee ranking members ($250,000), chief deputy whips ($250,000), ranking members ($200,000), and Appropriations

Committee and Ways and Means Committee members ($150,000) were all expected to raise more money for the Democratic Party as a result of their respective positions.

There was widespread belief among the black and Latino members that they were subject to additional hurdles and burdens that their white colleagues did not face. That is, they suffered personal slights that often indicated a lack of inclusion in the process, despite exclusive committee status, committee ranking member status, caucus chair status, and so on. In roughly twenty interviews, members spoke of being overlooked by donors who readily gave money to others on their committee (including white Democrats). They also felt that they were either entirely excluded from policy negotiations, or dismissed during negotiation when attempting to advocate for their districts and their constituents back home.[17]

CONCLUSION

Coalitions, particularly progressive coalitions, play a pivotal role in the protection of marginalized groups, especially for minorities, women, the LGBT community, and the poor. Though this dynamic is seldom embraced by constituents in their districts, it is felt very acutely by certain legislators in Congress, especially those in the Democratic Caucus and members of the Congressional Black, Hispanic, and Asian Pacific American Caucuses. To say there is strength in numbers during the policy process would be an understatement. Contemporary policy outcomes heavily depend on the willingness of various groups to ally with one another and overcome a status quo that focuses on a more privileged mainstream.

One interesting aspect of this research is the implication for majority-minority districts. If intersectional racism is occurring at the collective level of government, and directed toward districts and not just individual legislators, does that constitute an argument against majority-minority districts? It could, but it ignores the more insidious nature of racism itself. Rearranging minority neighborhoods may lead to lowered levels of descriptive representation, as well as lowered feelings of efficacy among minority groups, who have historically been excluded from the political process. With lower levels of descriptive representation, we would run the risk of jeopardizing the quality of deliberation in the legislative branch. Moreover, there is little evidence to suggest that adding more whites to a district would result in a greater chance of minority issues being addressed. That is, in districts with larger white populations, members offer less support for civil rights issues, even controlling for partisan status.

Another interesting aspect is the personal location of oneself in relation to past discrimination or exclusion, and the role that plays in the process of identity as an advocate for civil rights. If support for civil rights is dependent upon a personal experience of discrimination, or a willingness to believe another person's experience is different than one's own, this puts minorities at a strong disadvantage. That is, when a larger mainstream has not had experiences that could help develop empathy and understanding of rather pervasive societal prejudice, then minority legislators are ill-equipped to combat it through policy if their colleagues are unwilling to believe them.

Joint events hosted by all three of the minority caucuses are increasingly prominent both on the Hill and off. Those public events hosted on Capitol Hill are well attended by members of all three caucuses, while members look forward to events like the annual Tri-Caucus Health Summit, and other functions geared to addressing the particular needs of various communities that have been overlooked. As members work together and continue to promote interracial coalitions in the House, we can expect to see stronger patterns of support.

Conclusion

What's important is *not* how many black legislators we have, it's
the Democrats being in control.

                —Member 12, White, South

I definitely, without question, believe that we are linked and
that the ability of the Hispanic community to raise issues comes
from the fight and the loss of life and the deprivation of African
Americans in this country.

                —Member 11, Black, Midwest

In the House of Representatives, the ability for legislators from and representing marginalized communities—including, but not limited to, racial
minorities, women, the LGBT community, and the poor—to successfully
advocate on behalf of their constituencies requires participation in a process marked by contingencies and contrary interests. Success depends on
the individual skill to forge steadfast alliances that prioritize the distinct
needs and interests of those who have been historically excluded from national elite social structures. Therein lies the crux of this matter: successful advocacy for marginal groups necessarily requires political elites to
coalesce and champion the needs and interests of those who have systematically been excluded from their own ranks. In a political arena where
behavior is often motivated by expedience and self-interest rather than
principle, this is an exceedingly daunting task.

Considerable nuance shapes and propels the members of the recently assembled Congressional Tri-Caucus, in that this coalition of members from racially marginalized backgrounds is uniquely informed by personal experience (both past and present). In essence, the shared experience of marginalization across racial barriers has led to a more permanent alliance between the members of the Congressional Asian Pacific American, Black, and Hispanic Caucuses. Their continued cooperation reflects a new phase for minority representation at the federal level.

Certain background events cannot be omitted from this assessment, however. The most prominent being the partisan break that occurred during the late 1990s in the Hispanic Caucus. While the caucus operated as a bipartisan entity for more than two decades, some infighting occurred due to partisan and ideological differences that could not be reconciled. That split, when Hispanic Republicans in Congress formed the Congressional Hispanic Conference, resulted in a much more progressive caucus membership, which in turn provided an opportunity for alliances with the notably more liberal Black and Asian Pacific American Caucuses. Without that partisan separation, the three caucuses likely would not have united.

Although increased descriptive representation in the House of Representatives has contributed to deliberative improvements intended to benefit marginal groups, the members of the Congressional Tri-Caucus face continued resistance in the House of Representatives and more subtle opposition in the Senate, where those members from the same political party are often more conservative, both in terms of ideology and in terms of legislative approach.[1] The Senate remains much smaller in number and considerably less diverse than the lower chamber. Moreover, the institutional rules governing the Senate require far greater levels of consensus than those of the House of Representatives. All of these dynamics contribute to a sort of dilution of racial minority influence in the legislative process. During the course of my interviews, a significant number of Tri-Caucus members lamented the willingness of the Senate to remove language and provisions from bills that would benefit struggling communities. They offered that the conference process, which usually included prominent representatives from the House, the Senate, and the presidential administration, would drop language specifically included in the House version to benefit communities at risk. As such, the positive legislative power of members from and representing these communities was often rendered wholly ineffective during the later stages of the process.

As difficult as it is to create and implement substantive policy change through the legislative process, it is equally if not more difficult to undo the negative impact of past policies put into effect by legislatures that collectively had a more apathetic disposition to the needs and interests of marginal groups. In essence, overriding the often problematic status quo requires tremendous positive legislative power that representative advocates have yet to achieve concurrently in both chambers of Congress and in the executive branch. And, the status quo frequently lends to the cumulative inequality of American society. Perhaps more controversial, "conservative" regimes led by congressional leaders such as Newt Gingrich, Dick Armey, Dennis Hastert, Tom Delay, and a host of others initiated policies that led to levels of income and wealth inequality unseen since the 1920s.

To overcome the odds, members of the Tri-Caucus have focused on their common experiences and a perception of a linked fate that exists not only within each pan-ethnic racial group, but also among them. I have named this perception *linked political fate*. It exists both inside and outside of the legislative process, but it is most acutely felt by those attempting to advocate for and from racially marginalized communities. Moreover, many of the members of the House of Representatives from and representing racial minority communities contend that the linked fate extends far beyond "consensus" issues of race, to cross-cutting issues such as poverty, gender, and sexual orientation.

The question remains whether this alliance in federal politics will promote increased levels of racial understanding at the state and local levels. Researchers have found that constituents often take political cues from elites when it comes to race relations (Telles et al. 2011). In certain metropolitan areas, notably Los Angeles, contemporary political activity seems encouraging—organizations such as Community Coalition bolster civic engagement and multiracial organizing for progressive change. Elected officials at the city, county, and state level (including leaders from and representing black, Latino, and Asian American communities) stress the need to "break walls down" rather than build them up.[2]

RETHINKING THE REDISTRICTING PROCESS
AND ELECTORAL SELECTION

The potential shift toward maximizing influence districts in state redistricting processes may result in political outcomes exactly opposite to proponents' desires. Ideally, race would not have enough salience to prevent white citizens from voting with minorities. That said, the dynamic of group threat presents a serious challenge to the goals of the Democrats who sponsored the new redistricting procedure, as well as other "liberals" who believe race should be taken less into account. For instance, while a district with a 15-percent minority population may not trigger group threat among the majority, a 35-percent minority population might. As such, very close attention must be paid to levels of racial polarization when shaping legislative districts. In *Southern Politics* (1949), V.O. Key made clear that in the South, where historically black populations were the highest and slavery flourished, whites bore a long history of perpetuating white supremacy and domination. In essence, increased minority presence contributed to group threat and racial oppression. The white political elite of the South took great effort to prevent minorities from achieving political gains long after blacks were officially granted the right to vote.

Kinder and Sanders offer substantial evidence to suggest that white support for racial policies is significantly impacted by *perceptions* of group threat. Self-interest may be replaced by group interest as the most salient factor in assessing racial policy preferences, and political behavior may follow suit. Moreover, perception of threat is highly correlated with feelings of racial resentment (1996).

As the great migration carried blacks out of the rural South into the cities, South and North, miniature black belts were created everywhere. And time and time again, as the black share of the population increased, whites became more reactionary in their views on race. (Kinder and Sanders 1996, 82)

Sidanius et al. (2000) argue that the desire for group dominance is among the most important motives underlying opposition to race-specific policies. One's position in a racial hierarchy is a powerful indicator of egalitarian beliefs. Members of a dominant racial group are "less committed to the value of equality" than traditionally subordinate groups, such as blacks and Latinos (227).

Research also suggests that white voters are easily manipulated by implicit racial messages employed by campaigns to trigger subconscious hostility toward blacks.[3] Voters are primed with negative stereotypes about African Americans and other minority groups, and campaigns are known to manipulate voter behavior by generating anti-black sentiments among voters (Mendelberg 2001).[4]

One has to wonder whether a representative of an influence district can adequately represent the needs of his or her minority constituents without the fear of triggering white resentment, group threat, and consequent backlash. In these new districts, minority representatives find themselves in a highly precarious position. On the one hand, as a lawmaker, a representative has the opportunity to create effective policy change. On the other hand, should a representative seem too sympathetic to racialized issues (such as welfare and affirmative action), conservative white voters in the district may organize to unseat the representative.

One argument made in numerous political circles contends that a tradeoff occurred with the increased number of black and Latino representatives beginning in 1992. That is, traditionally Democratic minority voters were moved out of districts with white Democratic representation, and as a result, white Republicans were elected as the new representatives of those districts in 1994. This change, in turn, led to Republican control of the House. Still others argue that this "Republican Revolution" had little to do with the increases in descriptive representation, and more with an increasingly conservative tide in American politics that had been brewing for years before 1994. Whether or not there was a causal relationship, it is rather intriguing that only two years after the most sizable gains in minority representation in the history of Congress, the party more often in opposition to civil rights (in recent decades) came into power, and then controlled the House for twelve years.

The white elephant in the room, however, tends to be the nature of racial polarization itself. I assert this not to imply that scholars have not documented racial disparities in public opinion, but rather to suggest that so much time and energy is utilized with the hope that minorities will have a distinct impact on public policy, but so little time and energy is spent trying to break down the racial barriers that contribute to the persistence of racial inequality. Many members of the Tri-Caucus conveyed that this breakdown was an ultimate goal, particularly among blacks and Latinos, though they worried about the "divide and conquer" tactics of outside groups. That said, most of those who spoke fervently for the need for multiracial coalitions also made it clear that building those bridges is their responsibility as elected leaders of the community. They feel that it is incumbent upon them to take an active role in facilitating dialogue and conversation between the groups, and making sure that their words and deeds are congruent.

In another vein, we have to question whether the current electoral process[5] produces optimal outcomes. That is, many other entities within corporate and educational institutions allow voters to rank their preferences and employ instant runoff voting. In instant runoff voting, should a voter's first preference come in last, then their vote goes to their second preference. Should their second preference come in last, their vote is distributed to their third preference, and so on. This process increases the likelihood that a majority of the population would have a representative that they prefer. And, such a process would encourage cooperation and consensus-building among candidates and would-be lawmakers, rather than polarization.

THE TORTOISE AND THE HARE

One of the foundational premises of this book is the notion that the continued Republican marginalization of legislative advocates for marginal groups bolstered and solidified alliances across racial divides and resulted in steadfast progressive alliances. The Congressional Tri-Caucus comprises well over 25 percent of the Democratic Caucus in the House, and now has members who have gained the seniority necessary to create substantive policy change, should the Democrats hold a majority.

An equally important point to make is that the Republican strategy of racial exclusion seems unsustainable in the long term. That is, in the short term, the so-called "Southern Strategy," where elites exploit racial cleavages as a means to incite white hostility toward other groups (initially through overt means, and more recently with the use of psychological priming and subtle cues) has been a highly successful mobilizing factor in Republican electoral gains over the last five decades. Nevertheless, the same strategy that initially served as a catalyst for Republican political dominance may work to their detriment in the long run. Increased levels of racial liberalization, immigrant influx, and positive interracial interaction have resulted in increases in racial minority populations and consequent vote strength. As population and voter demographics change, so too will the makeup of popularly elected legislators. Many tactics embraced by conservatives to suppress minority turnout during elections have increasingly become ineffective. That is, while they may have demonstrable success in the near future, that effect is no longer great enough to stymie the increased turnout correlating with other national demographic shifts. In effect, with the politics of exclusion manifested through an anti-egalitarian platform, the Republican Party has inadvertently created an increasingly resistant force that opposes their agenda.

Notes on Variables from Chapter 4

Voting Age Population (by race): Census 2000. The total voting age population was calculated by the following groups: white males and females; black males and females; American Indian/Alaskan Native (AIAN) males and females; Native Hawaiian/Pacific Islander (NHPI) males and females Asian males and females; Other males and females; and males and females of two or more races. The Hispanic group is spread across all ethnicities (one could be a white Hispanic or a black Hispanic, for example), so this number was not included in the total voting age population, but rather the percentage of the voting age population that is Hispanic is included. My numbers reflect changes in the Texas congressional districts following their controversial redistricting that occurred during the middle of the 2000–10 decade, and the consequent changes after the Supreme Court of the United States overturned certain district boundaries.

Voting age population (by gender): Census 2000. The percent of the voting age population by gender (male/female).

Education: Census 2000. The population aged twenty-five years and over was calculated by district, based on 2000 census information. Then, the percent of that group that graduated from high school, and the percent that graduated from college was calculated for each district.

South: Whether a district is located in one of the Southern states of: Alabama, Arkansas, Florida, Georgia, Kentucky, Louisiana, Mississippi,

North Carolina, South Carolina, Tennessee, Texas, Virginia, or West Virginia.

Urban: Census 2000. Percentage of the congressional district population residing in an urban area.

Income: Census 2000. Median household income by district, deflated by 1000.

108th Congress Traditional Civil Rights measures included: LCCR. H.R. 3030, H.R. 4766, H.R. 4754, H.R. 4204, H.R. 3313, H.R. 106, and H.R. 1261.

108th Congress Contemporary Social Welfare measures included: LCCR. H.R. 3214, H.R. 2210, H.R. 3722, H.R. 975, H.C.R. 95, H.R. 1308, H.R. 8, H.R. 3031, H.R. 5006, H.R. 444, H.R. 4, and H.R. 4 (amendment).

109th Congress Traditional Civil Rights measures included: H.R. 418, H.R. 27, H.R. 3070, H.R. 3132, H.R. 1461, H.R. 4437, H.R. 4939 (Millender-McDonald Amendment), H.R. 609, H.R. 5441, H.R. 9 (including all amendments), H.J. Res. 88, H.R. 2389, H.R. 4844, and H.R. 2679.

109th Congress Contemporary Social Welfare measures included: H.R. 2123, H.R. 3010, H.R. 4241, H.R. 4939 (Capuano Amendment), and H.R. 609 (Democratic Substitute).

Race of Representative: *Almanac of American Politics.*

Party of Representative: *Almanac of American Politics.*

Gender of Representative: *Almanac of American Politics.*

DemSouth: The interaction effect of the two dummy variables: Location in the Southern region of the United States * Whether the member is a member of the Democratic Caucus. (Democratic caucus membership includes Bernie Sanders of Vermont, who was an independent until 2015, at which time he officially registered as a Democrat.)

Models of Majority Black, Latino Districts and Influence Districts

Here I include additional models that focus solely on majority black districts, black influence districts, majority Latino districts and Latino influence districts in the US House of Representatives. Table B1 includes districts that have black majorities or black influence (without regard to the Hispanic population) in the 108th Congress. Table B2 includes districts that have Latino majorities or Latino influence (without regard to the black population) in the 108th Congress. Table B3 includes black majority and influence districts for the 109th Congress. Table B4 includes Latino majority and Latino influence districts for the 109th Congress.

Table B1 Tobit Estimates of the Effect of District/Legislator Characteristics on % Legislator Support for Civil Rights Legislation, Black Majority/Influence Districts, 108th Congress

Independent Variable	LCCR Total Score	Traditional Civil Rights	Social Welfare
District Characteristics			
Black Majority	5.936	28.513	1.801
	(6.944)	(17.266)	(7.459)
Black Influence	3.182	23.642	2.161
	(4.885)	(13.020)	(5.144)
South	−15.157***	−36.745***	−14.943***
	(2.018)	(6.007)	(2.118)
Income (deflated by $1000)	−.602***	−1.013*	−.609***
	(.145)	(.401)	(.153)
Education	56.562***	130.628**	57.746**
	(17.215)	(48.141)	(18.256)
Urban	22.987***	65.698***	15.631**
	(5.462)	(14.962)	(5.745)
Representative Characteristics			
Democrat	75.961***	127.475***	75.784***
	(1.953)	(6.672)	(2.068)
Race (Black)	−7.914	−37.317*	−2.750
	(5.838)	(14.691)	(6.263)
Constant	13.887**	−47.421***	22.125***
	(4.991)	(14.425)	(5.256)
Number of Observations	434	434	434
Pseudo R^2	.8672	.8175	.8607

NOTE: Numbers in parentheses are standard errors.

*p < .05, **p < .01, ***p < .001.

Table B2 TOBIT ESTIMATES OF THE EFFECT OF DISTRICT/LEGISLATOR CHARACTERISTICS ON % LEGISLATOR SUPPORT FOR CIVIL RIGHTS LEGISLATION, LATINO MAJORITY/INFLUENCE DISTRICTS, 108TH CONGRESS

Independent Variable	LCCR Total Score	Traditional Civil Rights	Social Welfare
District Characteristics			
Latino Majority	3.897	33.310	−.780
	(8.388)	(20.603)	(8.840)
Latino Influence	2.897	6.839	.498
	(4.237)	(11.031)	(4.448)
South	−15.284***	−36.500***	−15.001***
	(1.993)	(5.847)	(2.101)
Income (deflated by $1000)	−.571***	−.847*	−.603***
	(.141)	(.386)	(.150)
Education	65.711***	155.660**	64.451***
	(17.854)	(49.848)	(18.958)
Urban	16.807**	40.773**	12.114*
	(5.736)	(15.548)	(6.066)
Representative Characteristics			
Democrat	75.250***	125.316***	75.441***
	(1.894)	(6.478)	(2.011)
Race (Latino)	5.672	−2.398	8.676
	(8.347)	(20.350)	(8.816)
Constant	14.784**	−42.574**	22.808***
	(4.974)	(14.254)	(5.247)
Number of Observations	434	434	434
Pseudo R^2	.8686	.8221	.8611

NOTE: Numbers in parentheses are standard errors.

*p < .05, **p < .01, ***p < .001.

Table B3 TOBIT ESTIMATES OF THE EFFECT OF DISTRICT/LEGISLATOR
CHARACTERISTICS ON % LEGISLATOR SUPPORT FOR CIVIL RIGHTS
LEGISLATION, BLACK MAJORITY/INFLUENCE DISTRICTS, 109TH CONGRESS

Independent Variable	LCCR Total Score	Traditional Civil Rights	Social Welfare
District Characteristics			
Black Majority	−.718	.668	−5.896
	(7.233)	(7.571)	(17.349)
Black Influence	−.337	.368	−3.073
	(5.216)	(5.427)	(11.082)
South	−17.113***	−18.098***	−22.648
	(2.204)	(2.293)	(4.675)
Income (deflated by $1000)	−.440**	−.458**	−.547
	(.160)	(.167)	(.351)
Education	50.307**	50.665*	78.153
	(19.074)	(19.821)	(44.162)
Urban	25.885***	29.297***	24.604
	(6.026)	(6.266)	(13.118)
Representative Characteristics			
Democrat	71.581***	67.519***	113.218
	(2.190)	(2.279)	(5.758)
Race (Black)	2.497	2.259	3.312
	(5.846)	(6.077)	(14.129)
Constant	13.232	14.456*	8.178
	(5.423)	(5.640)	(11.500)
Number of Observations	435	435	435
Pseudo R^2	.8366	.8153	.7878

NOTE: Numbers in parentheses are standard errors.

$p < .05$, **$p < .01$, ***$p < .001$.

Table B4 Tobit Estimates of the Effect of District/Legislator Characteristics on % Legislator Support for Civil Rights Legislation, Latino Majority/Influence Districts, 109th Congress

Independent Variable	LCCR Total Score	Traditional Civil Rights	Social Welfare
District Characteristics			
Latino Majority	5.344	7.830	−3.820
	(8.889)	(9.188)	(21.686)
Latino Influence	6.331	6.240	16.206
	(4.741)	(4.918)	(11.598)
South	−17.029***	−18.010***	−22.583
	(2.167)	(2.251)	(4.635)
Income (deflated by $1000)	−.445**	−.469**	−.495
	(.157)	(.164)	(.346)
Education	62.031**	63.835**	93.693
	(19.845)	(20.599)	(45.396)
Urban	21.155***	24.165***	15.079
	(6.345)	(6.597)	(13.745)
Representative Characteristics			
Democrat	71.527***	67.552***	112.419
	(2.106)	(2.190)	(5.499)
Race (Latino)	4.754	3.557	22.342
	(8.686)	(8.958)	(22.971)
Constant	13.700*	15.133**	8.309
	(5.412)	(5.622)	(11.474)
Number of Observations	435	435	435
Pseudo R^2	.8378	.8174	.7863

NOTE: Numbers in parentheses are standard errors.

*$p < .05$, **$p < .01$, ***$p < .001$.

CHAPTER 1

1. Particularly for women and racial minorities including African Americans, Asian Americans, Latinos, and Native Americans.
2. The delegates from the District of Columbia, American Samoa, Northern Mariana Islands, Guam, and the Virgin Islands, along with the Res. Commissioner from Puerto Rico do not have voting privileges on the floor of the House of Representatives.
3. This case was heard in a federal district court, but not challenged by Anne Arundel County.
4. This definition is provided by Davidson (1992). A similar definition can be found in Engstrom and MacDonald (1987).
5. Most notably African Americans, though research on pan-Latino perceptions of linked fate is emerging in the social sciences.

CHAPTER 2

1. This also includes, but is not limited to, literature on congressional behavior, institutional change, racial minority group politics, and marginal group politics.
2. At times this analysis can be more broadly applied to state and local governments. In other instances, it is specific to the internal structures of Congress and the House in particular. Relationships between groups are highly contextual, and have been transformed over the years by the willingness of political elites to effectively address inter-group tensions. This is also highly contextual depending upon the proximity of the governmental entity to the neighborhoods and localities represented. That is, legislators at the federal level work with larger budgets, and have greater opportunity to create a positive-sum relationship between constituent subgroups. Similarly, spatial distance from one's district (for most members of Congress, Washington, DC is much farther from home than city hall or a state capitol) may mean more emotional and psychological distance from intergroup tension and racial competition.
3. From *The Boundaries of Blackness: AIDS and the Breakdown of Black Politics* (1999), Chapters 1, 2.

4. This may also extend to the growing number of Asian American legislators, particularly in the Pacific region.
5. There are, however, extremely important contributions to note, including Rogers Smith's work on citizenship and social constructions of "Americanism," Paul Frymer's work on the two-party structure and the tenuous relationship between blacks and the Democratic Party, and Katherine Tate's research on the impact of African American members of Congress, just to name a few.
6. It is important to note that the nature of discrimination in Congress has changed considerably since the 1950s and 1960s, when Southern Democratic chairs were openly hostile to racial minority members. There has been a huge difference in the treatment of African American representatives since the 1960s. Overt, public racism is seldom an issue.
7. This argument is neither an endorsement nor a disavowal of current redistricting processes, particularly the emphasis of majority-minority districts and influence districts. Moreover, it should not be interpreted as a criticism of the geographical district model of representation. Rather, it is an opportunity to note the potential dynamics that occur in group settings, and the compounded effects of marginality in the legislative arena.
8. Adoption of these myths need not be a conscious decision. To the contrary, work in the fields of psychology and political psychology suggests that a significant amount of racial, class, and gender stereotypes occur at the subconscious level. Conscious or subconscious, pernicious racial stereotypes can still affect the behavior and attitudes of everyday individuals.
9. Schwarz, Alan. 2007. "Study of N.B.A. Sees Racial Bias in Calling Fouls." *New York Times*, May 2.
10. In Chapter 5, I will explore this in greater depth, relying on interviews with various members of the House of Representatives.
11. This is not to say that poor whites and middle-class minorities do not suffer from class and race prejudice, or to suggest that their experience is not important. Both types of prejudice can be extremely pernicious and can have a sizable impact on one's life chances. My point is that the intersection of multiple types of oppression and marginalization, combined with the geographic concentration of those oppressions, presents a heightened dilemma in the legislative process.
12. This point will be further explored in Chapter 5.
13. A more thorough review of research on black representation can be found in Chapter 4.
14. This number changed when Rep. Juanita Millender-McDonald (D-CA) passed away in April 2007.
15. The following committees were included in the tally: Agriculture, Appropriations, Armed Services, Education and Labor, Energy, Financial Services, Foreign Affairs, Homeland Security, Judiciary, Natural Resources, Oversight and Government Reform, Rules, Science and Technology, Small Business, Transportation and Infrastructure, Veterans' Affairs, Ways and Means, and the Select Committee on Intelligence. The total for the CBC subcommittee chairs included non-floor-voting members Eleanor Holmes Norton, Delegate from the District of Columbia, and

Donna Christian-Christiansen, Delegate from the US Virgin Islands. In addition, Eni Faleomavega (D-Samoa), Madeleine Bordallo (D-Guam), and David Wu (D-OR), all of the Congressional Asian Pacific American Caucus (CAPAC), became subcommittee chairs. Rep. Bobby Scott (D-VA), who is multiracial and caucuses with both the Asian Pacific Islander Caucus and the Black Caucus, is included in the CBC tally, having gained chairmanship of the Subcommittee on Crime, Terrorism and Homeland Security of the Judiciary Committee.

16. This seems fairly universal for members of Congress, regardless of the racial background of the member or his or her constituents. While districts with larger populations of racial minorities tend to be poorer that those of their white counterparts, concentrated poverty and economic depression in any district will require greater attention to the immediate needs of the constituency.

17. To be clear, there are very few issues that affect any community universally. The dominance of certain groups in agenda-setting reflects an imbalance of the needs being adequately addressed.

18. Dawson's original view on linked fate was a psychological-cognitive approach to the role of identity in grassroots voting behavior. This argument is an extension of this logic, applied to the conscious strategies of elected officials as they navigate identity and group politics in legislatures. My argument implies a less affective approach to politics than Dawson's cognitive model suggests, instead focusing on the conscious strategies utilized as a reaction to a long history of group competition in US policy.

19. This has not always been the case in the past, particularly when black leaders had the opportunity in the 1980s and early 1990s to speak out against homophobia-driven policy toward AIDS prevention. In turn, failure to support AIDS prevention through medical research, combined with an unwillingness to educate their communities about HIV/AIDS, has contributed to higher levels of the disease in black communities.

20. This is actually derived from my empirical research. It is based on knowledge obtained through interviewing more than forty members of Congress.

21. These ideas are well explored in chapter 6 of Hanna Pitkin's *The Concept of Representation* (1967).

22. This is not to suggest that members of Congress should only represent racially homogenous or nearly homogenous districts. It is more to suggest that the ability to respond to the needs of marginal groups in one's district can be significantly compromised when there is the presence of a dominant majority polarized against the minority.

23. In this case, the minority party was the Democratic Party.

24. From the *Congressional Record*, September 29, 2006, page H8027. Incidentally, this piece of Homeland Security legislation included nongermane restrictions on Internet gambling.

25. For examples, we can look to the statewide campaigns of Rep. Harold Ford, Jr. (D-TN), who ran for US Senate from Tennessee in the 2006 general election, and Rep. Artur Davis (D-AL), who ran for Governor of Alabama in 2010, losing in the primary race. Both positioned themselves as conservative "Blue Dog" Democrats,

despite the preferences (and ostensibly the interests) of their largely impoverished, African American constituencies.

CHAPTER 3

1. Sidney George Fisher, conservative lawyer from Philadelphia, post-Civil War, at
    the beginning of Reconstruction.
2. Notable exceptions include, but are not limited to, Swain 1993; Lublin 1997;
    Canon 1999; and Tate 2003.
3. Notable exceptions include Lieberman, King, Katznelson, Smith, and Parker.
4. 92 U.S. 214, 217–218 (1875).
5. 92 U.S. 542, 566 (1876).
6. *Guinn v. United States* (1915) 238 U.S. 347.
7. 163 US 537.
8. Women, regardless of ethnicity, would not be granted the right to vote until en-
    actment of the Nineteenth Amendment on August 18, 1920.
9. Laney, Garrine. 2006. "The Voting Rights Act of 1965, As Amended: Its History and
    Current Issues." *Congressional Research Service* (CRS). Order Code 95-896 GOV.
10. *Congressional Record*, vol. 68, part 5, March 2, 1927, pp. 5361–5363.
11. 321 U.S. 649 (1944).
12. Emphasis mine.
13. 270 F. 2d 594, 611.; 364 U.S. 339 (1960).
14. P.L. 86-449; 74 Stat. 86.
15. This provision, of course, did not protect any number of language minorities in
    the US. This would later be addressed in the 1975 amendments to the VRA.
16. 369 U.S. 186 (1962).
17. 377 U.S. 533 (1964).
18. 376 U.S. 1 (1964).
19. 42 U.S.C. 1973, 1973b(f).
20. *South Carolina v. Katzenbach* (1966) 383 U.S. 301.
21. It is important to note here that little national attention was paid to the political
    abuses suffered by the Latino communities in the Southwest. This will be ad-
    dressed in subsequent sections of this chapter.
22. Including Augustus Hawkins, William Dawson, Charles Diggs, John Conyers,
    Adam Clayton Powell, and Robert Nix.
23. Though not affected by redistricting, Massachusetts also elected an African
    American, Edward Brooke, to the United States Senate in 1966 in a statewide
    election. Brooke would serve for two consecutive terms, as part of the liberal
    wing of the Republican Party, often conflicting with President Nixon over judicial
    issues and appointments.
24. This is not to suggest that there is not tremendous diversity within the black
    community of the United States; the categorical marginalization that African
    Americans have historically experienced in the US had a reductionist tendency
    from very early on, leading to a pan-ethnic identity that emerged centuries ago.
    The black experience in the United states is anything but monolithic, and there

is cultural variation particularly between descendents of US slaves versus blacks who hail from the Caribbean.

25. *Mendez v. Westminster*, 64 F.Supp. 544 (C.D. Cal. 1946), aff'd, 161 F.2d 774 (9th Cir. 1947) (en banc). This case was led by five Mexican families in Orange County, CA, who protested the segregation of their children's school.

26. 347 U.S. 475 (1954).

27. The group is occasionally referred to as "La Raza."

28. The exception being Joachim Fernandez (D-LA), who served from 1931 to 1941. This does not include the Resident Commissioners of Puerto Rico, who do not have floor-voting rights in the House of Representatives.

29. Chinese Americans currently comprise roughly 1.2% of the American populace, with roughly 3.8 million persons of Chinese ancestry currently residing in the US.

30. A number of these reforms, such as the Immigration Act of 1924, were also passed into law with the desire of shutting out Eastern and Southern Europeans.

31. The internment policy was for persons of "foreign enemy ancestry," and also included some 10,000 persons of German descent, and 3,000 Italian Americans.

32. House Subcommittee on Civil and Constitutional Rights, *Extension of the Voting Rights Act*, pp. 27–29, 519–535, 598–604, 800–828, 853–886, 922–932. Also, U.S. Congress, Senate, Committee on the Judiciary, Subcommittee on Constitutional Rights, *Extension of the Voting Rights Act of 1965*, hearings on S. 407 [and other bills], 94th Cong., 1st sess. (Washington: GPO, 1975), pp. 361–362, 1040–1041; U.S. Commission on Civil Rights, *The Voting Rights Act: Ten Years After*, Report, 1975 (Washington: GPO, 1975), p. 438.

CHAPTER 4

1. This quote is taken directly from the Supreme Court decision. 539 U.S. ___(2003), page 5.

2. Senator Robert Brown in the *Georgia v. Ashcroft* decision. 539 U.S. ___(2003), page 5.

3. Senator Charles Walker in the *Georgia v. Ashcroft* decision. 539 U.S. ___(2003), page 6.

4. This member represented a black influence district, and was very candid about the potential for legislative success in civil rights. His civil rights voting record, according to LCCR report cards, hovered around 70 percent for both the 108th and 109th Congresses.

5. My reason for using tobit is that it allows for better approximations when the upper and lower bounds of a dependent variable are limited. In this case, the dependent variable is in the form of percentage, and consequently the lower bound is 0, while the upper bound is 100.

6. The LCCR measure utilizes "Roll Call" floor votes on key issues throughout a given two-year term. Although some recent research has moved away from the use of roll call votes to discern the quality of congressional representation, floor votes are not obsolete. They remain very useful for comparing and contrasting voting behavior at an aggregate level, particularly by district type, over longer periods

of time. Roll-call votes provide evidence of various patterns that can be further investigated through semi-structured interviews with the members themselves.

7. In addition, I generated a number of variables, including an interaction effect for those members who are Democrats from the South, with the hopes of fleshing out the unique dynamic of a higher level of conservatism that exists in the region; an interaction effect for black and Latino Democrats (race*party); and black and Latino women (race*gender). Other district variables not included in the final model but explored in preliminary analysis include: female identification as a percent of the district population, language ability statistics, and poverty rates. I also explored representative gender identification as a function of their roll call behavior, but found no statistical significance throughout multiple types of regression analysis.

8. This does not mean that their deeds have consistently matched their words. For further exploration of this issue, see Paul Frymer. 1999. *Uneasy Alliances: Race and Party Competition in America*. Princeton, NJ: Princeton University Press.

9. Incidentally, this Representative was relatively new to the House of Representatives, and at this point did not enjoy the increased benefits of incumbency advantage (Member 29, Black, South).

CHAPTER 5

1. These numbers are based on the participation in the 114th Congress, and only include floor-voting members of each caucus. The number for the Congressional Asian Pacific American Caucus only includes the Executive Board, and not the associate membership. In addition, it does not include members of the Executive Board who have already been counted as members of the Congressional Black and Hispanic Caucuses.

2. Pitkin (1967) often refers to this as the "Mandate-Independence Controversy," where a representative acts independently or sees his or her representation as a mandate from constituents. This does not carry over into mutually exclusive alternatives, where the wants of the represented are diametrically opposed to their perceived best interests, from the perspective of the representative.

3. These findings correspond with the work in Lisa Garcia Bedolla's *Fluid Borders: Latino Power, Identity and Politics in Los Angeles* (2005), which finds that many second- and third-generation Latinos in the United States have chosen to try to distance themselves from their ethnic heritage due to high levels of stigmatization in US culture. Those who choose to embrace their ethnic background (similar to Kauffman's "pan-Latino affinity") show higher levels of participation, self-esteem, and identification with others facing discrimination.

4. Though during the winter and spring of 2007, with the newly Democratic leadership, Republicans were still less willing to participate than Democrats, including committee chairs and members of leadership.

5. This number is actually proportional to the number of women in the House during the 109th Congress. Women comprised roughly 16 percent of the Representatives in the House during the 109th Congress. Should eight women have participated, I would have been slightly above the proportionate number.

6. For clarification purposes: superwhite majority districts have a white voting-age population greater than or equal to 70 percent, black majority districts have a black voting age population greater than or equal to 50 percent, Latino majority districts have a Latino voting age population greater than or equal to 50 percent, and black/Latino majority districts have a voting age population greater than or equal to 50 percent. Influence districts have voting age populations ranging from 30 to 50 percent.

7. According to census data from 2000 (www.census.gov).

8. For instance, see Oliver and Shapiro, *Black Wealth/White Wealth: A New Perspective on Racial Inequality* (1995).

9. This measure derived from recent Leadership Conference on Civil Rights (LCCR) scores, which includes legislation affecting racial minorities, women, and the LGBT community. Certain groups that participate in the conference argue that not all of these categories should be included as civil rights, particularly LGBT issues, but the LCCR includes them nonetheless.

10. Two members interviewed were not asked the question due to time constraints.

11. By "straightforward voting behavior" I mean that these separate pieces of legislation were not attached to much larger bills as quasi-germane amendments, and the legislation was significantly clear in the wording about intended outcomes. Other bills I considered included an amendment to the Children's Safety Act (H.R. 3132), where the Local Law Enforcement Hate Crimes Prevention Act was attached and provided protections for the LGBT community in hate crimes, and the proposed immigration legislation, H.R. 4437, the "Border Protection, Antiterrorism and Illegal Immigration Control Act," which was an extremely complex piece of legislation that could be potentially misinterpreted and misconstrued.

12. One member voted "Present" while an additional ten are on record as "not voting."

13. Tri-Caucus members who voted for the Secure Fence Act included Reps. Bishop (D-GA), Corrine Brown (D-FL), Cardoza (D-CA), Costa (D-CA), Davis (D-AL), and Ford (D-TN).

14. Those who voted in favor included Reps. Bishop (D-GA), Cuellar (D-TX), Davis (D-AL), Ford (D-TN), Jefferson (D-LA), Ortiz (D-TX), D. Scott (D-GA), and Thompson (D-MS). Interestingly, all are members from the South, and at least four are representing districts in the "Deep South." It is also worth noting that two of the three Tri-Caucus members who supported both the fence and the gay marriage ban, would later run for statewide office in the south: Rep. Ford of Tennessee would run for US Senate in 2006 (subsequent loss in the general election); and Rep. Davis of Alabama would run for Governor in 2010 (lost in the Democratic primary).

15. One example offered was an exchange during a committee markup for the Homeland Security Committee.

16. Those expressing concerns about the Democratic Party apparatus numbered twelve, while an additional six expressed negative feelings toward Rep. Emanuel. (This information was unprompted in the interview questionnaire.)

17. This included every Latino participant and all but four of the black participants.

CHAPTER 6

1. Multiple Tri-Caucus members mentioned the conference process as a source of legislative losses, suggesting that Senators were likely to oppose or dismiss hard-fought provisions they had attained in the House.
2. Quoting State Senator Kevin de Leon in a public speech in San Jose, February 27, 2016. This statement refers both to Republican candidates who call for a wall along the US-Mexico border, as well as to the racial barriers that exist in contemporary politics.
3. To be clear here, all racial groups have voters who are easily manipulated by advertisements and campaign propaganda that consciously or subconsciously trigger resentment.
4. Issues such as immigration reform seem to be employed as a means to generate racial polarization as well.
5. Generally winner-take-all, in which the candidate with the most votes is considered the electoral victor.

REFERENCES

Appiah, K. Anthony, and Amy Guttman. 1996. *Color Conscious: The Political Morality of Race.* Princeton, NJ: Princeton University Press.

Ayres, Ian. 2001. *Pervasive Prejudice? Nontraditional Evidence of Race and Gender Discrimination.* Chicago: University of Chicago Press.

Ayres, Ian. 1991. "Fair Driving: Gender and Race Discrimination in Retail Car Negotiations." *Harvard Law Review* 104: 817–872.

Banaji, Mahzarin R. 2001. "Ordinary Prejudice." *Psychological Science Agenda* January/February: 8–11.

Banaji, Mahzarin R., and R. Bhaskar. 2000. "Implicit Stereotypes and Memory: The Bounded Rationality of Social Beliefs." In *Memory, Brain and Belief,* edited by Daniel Schacter and Elaine Scarry, 139–175. Cambridge, MA: Harvard University Press.

Banducci, Susan A., Todd Donovan, and Jeffrey A, Karp. 2004. "Minority Representation, Empowerment and Participation." *The Journal of Politics* 66 (May): 534–556.

Baron, Andrew Scott, and Mahzarin Banaji. 2006. "The Development of Implicit Attitudes: Evidence of Race Evaluations from Ages 6 and 10 and Adulthood." *Psychological Science* 17(1): 53–58.

Barreto, Matt A., Gary Segura, and Nathan Woods. 2004. "The Mobilizing Effect of Majority-Minority Districts on Latino Turnout." *American Political Science Review* 98 (February): 65–75.

Barone, Michael. 2003. *The Almanac of American Politics.* Washington, DC: National Journal Group.

Bejarano, Christina E. 2013. *The Latina Advantage: Gender, Race, and Political Success.* Austin: University of Texas Press.

Bejarano, Christina E. 2013. *The Latino Gender Gap in U.S. Politics.* New York: Routledge.

Blassingame, John W. 1979. *The Slave Community: Plantation Life in the Antebellum South,* rev. ed. New York: Oxford University Press.

Bloom, Jack M. 1987. *Class, Race, and the Civil Rights Movement.* Bloomington: Indiana University Press.

Bobo, Lawrence, and Franklin D. Gilliam, Jr. 1990. "Race, Sociopolitical Participation, and Black Empowerment." *American Political Science Review* 84 (June): 377–393.

Brown, Nadia. 2014. *Sisters in the Statehouse: Black Women and Legislative Decision Making.* Oxford: Oxford University Press.

Brown, Rupert. 2000. *Group Processes: Dynamics Within and Between Groups.* Oxford: Blackwell Publishing.

Browning, Rufus P., Dale Rogers Marshall, and David H. Tabb. 1984. *Protest is Not Enough: The Struggle of Blacks and Hispanics for Equality in Urban Politics.* Berkeley: University of California Press.

Bullock, Charles S., III. 1994. "Section 2 of the Voting Rights Act, Districting Formats, and the Election of African-Americans." *The Journal of Politics* 56 (November): 1098–1105.

Cameron, Charles, David Epstein, and Sharyn O'Halloran. 1996. "Do Majority-Minority Districts Maximize Substantive Black Representation in Congress?" *American Political Science Review* 90 (December): 794–812.

Canon, David T. 1999. *Race, Redistricting and Representation: The Unintended Consequences of Black Majority Districts.* Chicago: University of Chicago Press.

Carson, Clayborne. 1995. *In Struggle: SNCC and the Black Awakening of the 1960s.* Cambridge, MA: Harvard University Press.

Casellas, Jason P. 2011. *Latino Representation in State Houses and Congress.* Cambridge: Cambridge University Press.

Center for Responsive Politics. http://www.opensecrets.org.

Chafe, William H., Raymond Gavins, and Robert Korstad, eds. 2001. *Remembering Jim Crow: African-Americans Tell About Life in the Segregated South.* New York: The New Press.

Chong, Dennis. 1991. *Collective Action and the Civil Rights Movement.* Chicago: University of Chicago Press.

Clayton, Dewey M. 2000. *African Americans and the Politics of Congressional Redistricting.* New York: Garland Publishing, Inc.

Cohen, Cathy J. 1999. *The Boundaries of Blackness: AIDS and the Breakdown of Black Politics.* Chicago: University of Chicago Press.

Congressional Quarterly. 1993. *CQ's Guide to 1990 Congressional Redistricting.* Washington, DC: CQ Press.

Cox, Gary W., and Mathew D. McCubbins. 1993. *Legislative Leviathan: Party Government in the House.* Berkeley: University of California Press.

Cox, Gary W., and Mathew D. McCubbins. 1997. "Toward a Theory of Legislative Rules Changes: Assessing Schickler and Rich's Evidence." *American Journal of Political Science* 41 (October): 1376–1386.

Cox, Gary W., and Mathew D. McCubbins. 2005. *Setting the Agenda: Responsible Party Government in the U.S. House of Representatives.* Cambridge: Cambridge University Press.

Cox, Taylor H., Sharon A. Lobel, and Poppy Lauretta McLeod. 1991. "Effects of Ethnic Group Cultural Differences on Cooperative and Competitive Behavior on a Group Task." *Academy of Management Journal* 34: 827–847.

Cunningham, William A., John B. Nezlek, and Mahzarin Banaji. 2004. "Implicit and Explicit Ethnocentrism: Revisiting the Ideologies of Prejudice." *Personality and Social Psychology Bulletin* 30(10): 1332–1346.

Dahl, Robert A. 1956. *A Preface to Democratic Theory*. Chicago: University of Chicago Press.

Dahl, Robert. 1972. *Democracy in the United States: Promise and Performance*. Chicago: Rand McNally.

Darling, Marsha J. Tyson, ed. 2001. *Race, Voting, Redistricting and the Constitution: Sources and Explorations on the Fifteenth Amendment: Volume 1*. New York: Routledge.

Dasgupta, Nilanjana, Debbie E. McGhee, Anthony G. Greenwald, and Mazharin R. Banaji. 2000. "Automatic Preference for White Americans: Eliminating the Familiarity Explanation." *Journal of Experimental Social Psychology* 36: 316–328.

Davidson, Chandler, ed. 1989. *Minority Vote Dilution*. Washington, DC: Howard University Press.

Davidson, Chandler, and Bernard Grofman, eds. 1994. *Quiet Revolution in the South: The Impact of the Voting Rights Act 1965–1990*. Princeton, NJ: Princeton University Press.

Dawson, Michael C. 1994. *Behind the Mule: Race and Class in African-American Politics*. Princeton, NJ: Princeton University Press.

Dawson, Michael C., and Rovana Popoff. 2004. "Reparations: Justice and Greed in Black and White." *The Du Bois Review* 1: 47–92.

Devos, Thierry, and Mazharin Banaji. 2005. "American = White?" *Journal of Personality and Social Psychology* 88(3): 447–466.

Dodd, Lawrence C., and Bruce I. Oppenheimer. 2001. *Congress Reconsidered*, 7th ed. Washington, DC: CQ Press.

Douglass, Frederick. (1855). 1969. *My Bondage and My Freedom*. New York: Dover Publications, Inc.

DuBois, W.E.B. 1935. *Black Reconstruction in America: 1860–1880*. New York: Atheneum.

Dzidzienyo, Anani, and Suzanne Oboler, eds. 2005. *Neither Enemies nor Friends: Latinos, Blacks, Afro-Latinos*. New York: Palgrave MacMillan.

Epstein, David, and Sharyn O'Halloran. 1999. "Measuring the Electoral and Policy Impact of Majority-Minority Voting Districts." *American Journal of Political Science* 43 (April): 367–395.

Fair Vote. http://www.fairvote.org.

Feagin, Joe R. 2006. *Systemic Racism: A Theory of Oppression*. New York: Routledge.

Fenno, Richard F. 1978. *Home Style: House Members in their Districts*. New York: HarperCollins.

Fenno, Richard F. 1995. *Congressmen in Committees*, reprint ed. Berkeley: University of California Press.

Fenno, Richard F. 2003. *Going Home: Black Representatives and Their Constituents*. Chicago: University of Chicago Press.

Foner, Eric. 1990. *A Short History of Reconstruction*. New York: Harper and Row.

Franklin, John Hope, and Alfred A. Moss, Jr. 1994. *From Slavery to Freedom: A History of African Americans*, 7th ed. New York: McGraw-Hill, Inc.

Frymer, Paul. 1999. *Uneasy Alliances: Race and Party Competition in America*. Princeton, NJ: Princeton University Press.

Gamble, Katrine L. 2007. "Black Political Representation: An Examination of Legislative Activity Within U.S. House Committees." *Legislative Studies Quarterly* 32(3): 421–447.

Gay, Claudine. 2001. "The Effect of Black Congressional Representation on Political Participation." *American Political Science Review* 95 (September): 589–602.

Gilens, Martin. 1999. *Why Americans Hate Welfare: Race, Media and the Politics of Anti-Poverty Policy*. Chicago: University of Chicago Press.

Greenwald, Anthony G., Laurie A. Rudman, Brian A. Nosek, Mahzarin R. Banaji, Shelly D. Farnham, and Deborah S. Mellott. 2002. "A Unified Theory of Implicit Attitudes, Stereotypes, Self-Esteem and Self-Concept." *Psychological Review* 109(1): 3–25.

Grofman, Bernard, and Chandler Davidson, eds. *Controversies in Minority Voting: The Voting Rights Act in Perspective*. Washington, DC: The Brookings Institution.

Grofman, Bernard, and Lisa Handley. 1991. "The Impact of the Voting Rights Act on Black Representation in Southern State Legislatures." *Legislative Studies Quarterly* 16 (February): 111–128.

Grofman, Bernard, Lisa Handley, and David I. Lublin. 2001. "Drawing Effective Minority Districts: A Conceptual Framework and Some Empirical Evidence." *North Carolina Law Review* 79 (June): 1383–1430.

Grofman, Bernard, Lisa Handley, and Richard G. Niemi. 1992. *Minority Representation and the Quest for Voting Equality*. Cambridge: Cambridge University Press.

Grose, Christian R. 2011. *Congress in Black and White: Race and Representation in Washington and at Home*. Cambridge: Cambridge University Press.

Guinier, Lani. 1994. *The Tyranny of the Majority: Fundamental Fairness in Representative Democracy*. New York: Free Press.

Guinier, Lani, and Gerald Torres. 2002. *The Miner's Canary: Enlisting Race, Resisting Power, Transforming Democracy*. Cambridge, MA: Harvard University Press.

Hall, Richard L. 1996. *Participation in Congress*. New Haven, CT: Yale University Press.

Hall, Richard L., and Frank Wayman. 1990. "Buying Time: Moneyed Interests and the Mobilization of Bias in Congressional Committees." *The American Political Science Review* 84 (September): 797–820.

Hansen, John Mark. 1991. *Gaining Access: Congress and the Farm Lobby, 1919–1981*. Chicago: University of Chicago Press.

Hebert, J. Gerald, Donald B. Verilli, Jr., Paul M. Smith, and Sam Hirsch. 2000. *The Realists' Guide to Redistricting: Avoiding the Legal Pitfalls*. Chicago: American Bar Association.

Hero, Rodney E., and Robert Preuhs. 2013. *Black-Latino Relations in U.S. National Politics: Beyond Conflict or Cooperation*. Cambridge: Cambridge University Press.

Holt, Thomas. 1977. *Black Over White: Negro Political Leadership in South Carolina During Reconstruction*. Urbana: University of Illinois Press.

Holt, Thomas C. 2000. *The Problem of Race in the 21st Century*. Cambridge, MA: Harvard University Press.

Hutchings, Vincent L., Harwood K. McClerking, and Guy-Uriel Charles. 2004. "Congressional Representation of Black Interests: Recognizing the Importance of Stability." *The Journal of Politics* 66 (May): 450–468.

Jennings, James. 1992. *The Politics of Black Empowerment: The Transformation of Black Activism in America*. Detroit, MI: Wayne State University Press.

Jost, John T., Mahzarin R. Banaji, and Brian A. Nosek. 2004. "A Decade of System Justification Theory: Accumulated Evidence of Conscious and Unconscious Bolstering of the Status Quo." *Political Psychology* 25(6): 881–919.

Kaufmann, Karen. 2003. "Cracks in the Rainbow: Group Commonality as a Basis for Laino and African-American Political Coalitions." *Political Research Quarterly* 56(2): 199–210.

Kelley, Robin D. G. 2002. *Freedom Dreams: The Black Radical Imagination*. Boston: Beacon Press.

Key, V. O. 1949. *Southern Politics in State and Nation*. New York: Knopf.

Kim, Claire Jean. 2000. *Bitter Fruit: The Politics of Black-Korean Conflict in New York City*. New Haven, CT: Yale University Press.

Kinder, Donald, and Lynn Sanders. 1996. *Divided by Color: Racial Politics and Democratic Ideals*. Chicago: University of Chicago Press.

Krehbiel, Keith. 1998. *Pivotal Politics: A Theory of U.S. Lawmaking*. Chicago: University of Chicago Press.

Kymlicka, Will. 1995. *The Rights of Minority Cultures*. Oxford: Oxford University Press.

The Leadership Conference. http://www.civilrights.org/.

Lubiano, Wahneema, ed. *The House That Race Built: Black Americans, U.S. Terrain*. New York: Pantheon Books.

Lublin, David. 1997. *The Paradox of Representation*. Princeton, NJ: Princeton University Press.

Lublin, David. 1999. "Racial Redistricting and African-American Representation: A Critique of 'Do Majority Minority Districts Maximize Substantive Black Representation in Congress?'" *American Political Science Review* 93 (March): 183–186.

Mansbridge, Jane. 1999. "Should Blacks Represent Blacks and Women Represent Women? A Contingent 'Yes.'" *Journal of Politics* 61 (3): 628–657.

Massey, Douglas, and Nancy Denton. 1993. *American Apartheid: Segregation and the Making of the Underclass*. Cambridge, MA: Harvard University Press.

Mayhew, David R. 1974. *Congress: The Electoral Connection*. New Haven, CT: Yale University Press.

McAdam, Doug. 1982. *Political Process and the Development of Black Insurgency, 1930–1970*. Chicago: University of Chicago Press.

McClain, Paula. 2006. "Racial Intergroup Relations in a Set of Cities: A Twenty Year Perspective." *Journal of Politics* 68 (4): 757–770.

McClain, Paula, and Albert K. Karnig. 1990. "Black and Hispanic Socioeconomic and Political Competition." *American Political Science Review* 84 (June): 535–545.

Menchaca, Martha. 2001. *Recovering History, Constructing Race: The Indian, Black, and White Roots of Mexican Americans*. Austin: University of Texas Press.

Mendelberg, Tali. 2001. *The Race Card: Campaign Strategy, Implicit Messages and the Norm of Equality*. Princeton, NJ: Princeton University Press.

Messick, David M., and Diane M. Massie. 1989. "Intergroup Relations." *Annual Review of Psychology* 40: 45–81.

Mills, Charles W. 1997. *The Racial Contract*. Ithaca, NY: Cornell University Press.

Mindiola, Tatcho, Jr., Yolanda Flores Niemann, and Nestor Rodriguez. *Black-Brown Relations and Stereotypes*. Austin: University of Texas Press.

Minta, Michael D. 2011. *Oversight: Representing the Interests of Blacks and Latinos in Congress*. Princeton, NJ: Princeton University Press.

Minta, Michael D., and Valeria Sinclair-Chapman. 2013. "Diversity in Political Institutions and Congressional Responsiveness to Minority Interests." *Political Research Quarterly* 66 (1): 127–140.

Morris, Aldon D. 1984. *The Origins of the Civil Rights Movement: Black Communities Organizing for Change*. New York: The Free Press.

National Association for the Advancement of Colored People. http://www.naacp.org/.

Oliver, J. Eric, and Janelle Wong. 2003. "Intergroup Prejudice in Multiethnic Settings." *American Journal of Political Science* 47 (4): 567–582.

Oliver, Melvin L., and Thomas M. Shapiro. 1995. *Black Wealth/White Wealth: A New Perspective on Racial Inequality*. New York: Routledge.

O'Reilly, Charles A., III, Katherine Williams, and Sigal Barsade. 1998. "Group Demography and Innovation: Does Diversity Help?" *Research on Managing Groups and Teams* 1: 183–207.

Page-Gould, Elizabeth. 2007. *Causal Effects of Cross-Group Friendship: Understanding the Intergroup Benefits of Closeness Across Group Boundaries*. IPSR Colloquium: University of California Berkeley.

Palmer, Colin. 1998. *Passageways: An Interpretive History of Black America. Volume II: 1863–1965*. New York: Harcourt Brace.

Phillips, Katherine W. 2003. "The Effects of Categorically Based Expectations on Minority Influence: The Importance of Congruence." *Personality and Social Psychology Bulletin* 29 (January): 3–13.

Phillips, Katherine W., Elizabeth A. Mannix, Margaret A. Neale, and Deborah Gruenfeld. 2004. "Diverse Groups and Information Sharing: The Effects of Congruent Ties." *Journal of Experimental Social Psychology* 40: 497–510.

Phillips, Katherine W., and Denise Lewin Loyd. 2006. "When Surface and Deep-Level Diversity Collide: The Effects on Dissenting Group Members." *Organizational Behavior and Human Decision Processes* 99: 143–160.

Phillips, Katherine W., Gregory B. Northcraft, and Margaret A. Neale. 2006. "Surface Level Diversity and Decision-Making in Groups: When Does Deep-Level Similarity Help?" *Group Processes and Intergroup Relations* 9: 467–482.

Pildes, Richard. 2002. "Is Voting Rights Law Now at War With Itself? Social Science and Voting Rights in the 2000s." *North Carolina Law Review* 80 (June 2002): 1517–1573.

Pitkin, Hanna. 1967. *The Concept of Representation*. Berkeley: University of California Press.

Price, David E. 2004. *The Congressional Experience*. 3d ed. Cambridge, MA: Westview Press.

Rich, Wilbur C., ed. 1996. *The Politics of Minority Coalitions: Race, Ethnicity and Shared Uncertainties*. Westport, CT: Praeger.

Rivers, Christina R. 2012. *The Congressional Black Caucus, Minority Voting Rights, and the U.S. Supreme Court*. Ann Arbor: University of Michigan Press.

Rohde, David W. 1991. *Parties and Leaders in the Post Reform House*. Chicago: The University of Chicago Press.

Rosenbaum, David. 2002. "In Georgia, A Shot at Congress for Five Blacks." *New York Times* (September 24): A23.

Rosenberg, Gerald N. 1991. *The Hollow Hope: Can Courts Bring About Social Change?* Chicago: The University of Chicago Press.

Rosenstone, Steven J., and John Mark Hansen. 1993. *Mobilization, Participation and Democracy in America*. New York: Macmillan Publishing Company.

Rouse, Stella M. 2013. *Latinos in the Legislative Process: Interests and Influence*. Cambridge: Cambridge University Press.

Rush, Mark E., ed. 1998. *Voting Rights and Redistricting in the United States*. Westport, CT: Greenwood Press.

Schwarz, Alan. 2007. "Study of NBA Sees Racial Bias in Calling Fouls." *New York Times* (May 2).

Sears, David A., Jim Sidanius, and Lawrence Bobo. 2000. *Racialized Politics: The Debate About Racism in America*. Chicago: University of Chicago Press.

Scher, Richard K., Jon L. Mills, and John J. Hotaling. 1997. *Voting Rights and Democracy: The Law of Politics and Redistricting*. Chicago: Nelson-Hall Publishers.

Schickler, Eric. 2001. *Disjointed Pluralism: Institutional Innovation and the Development of the U.S. Congress*. Princeton, NJ: Princeton University Press.

Schickler, Eric, and Andrew Rich. 1997. "Party Government in the House Reconsidered: A Response to Cox and McCubbins." *American Journal of Political Science* 41 (October): 1387–1394.

Shepsle, Kenneth A., and Barry R. Weingast, eds. 1995. *Positive Theories of Congressional Institutions*. Ann Arbor: University of Michigan Press.

Sinclair, Barbara. 1983. "Purposive Behavior in the U.S. Congress: A Review Essay." *Legislative Studies Quarterly* 8 (February): 117–131.

Sinclair, Barbara. 1995. *Legislators, Leaders and Lawmaking: The U.S. House of Representatives in the Postreform Era*. Baltimore: Johns Hopkins Press.

Sinclair, Barbara. 1997. *Unorthodox Lawmaking: New Legislative Processes in the U.S. Congress*. Washington, DC: CQ Press.

Sitkoff, Harvard. 1993. *The Struggle for Black Equality 1954–1992*. revised ed. New York: Harper Collins.

Smith, Rogers. 1997. *Civic Ideals: Conflicting Visions of Citizenship in U.S. History*. New Haven, CT: Yale University Press.

Strolovitch, Dara. 2006. "Do Interest Groups Represent the Disadvantaged? Advocacy at the Intersections of Race, Class and Gender." *Journal of Politics* 68 (Nov): 894–910.

Strolovitch, Dara. 2007. *Affirmative Advocacy: Race, Class, and Gender in Interest Group Politics*. Chicago: University of Chicago Press.

Swain, Carol. 1993. *Black Faces, Black Interests: The Representation of African-Americans in Congress*. Cambridge, MA: Harvard University Press.

Tate, Katherine. 1994. *From Protest to Politics: The New Black Voters in American Elections*. Cambridge, MA: Harvard University Press.

Tate, Katherine. 2003. *Black Faces in the Mirror: African-Americans and Their Representatives in the U.S. Congress*. Princeton, NJ: Princeton University Press.

Tate, Katherine. 2014. *Concordance: Black Lawmaking in the U.S. Congress from Carter to Obama*. Ann Arbor: University of Michigan Press.

Taylor, Charles. 1994. *Multiculturalism: Examining the Politics of Recognition*. Princeton, NJ: Princeton University Press.

Telles, Edward, Mark Q. Sawyer, and Gaspar Rivera-Salgado, eds. 2011. *Just Neighbors? Research on African American and Latino Relations in the United States*. New York: Russell Sage.

United States Census Bureau. http://www.census.gov.

United States Department of Justice. "Voting Section." http://www.usdoj.gov/crt/voting/.

Vaca, Nicolas C. 2004. *The Presumed Alliance: The Unspoken Conflict between Latinos and Blacks and What It Means For America*. New York: Harper Collins.

Walton, Jr., Hanes. 1988. *When the Marching Stopped: The Politics of Civil Rights Regulatory Agencies*. Albany: State University of New York Press.

Williams, Katherine Y., and Charles A. O'Reilly, III. "Demography and Diversity in Organizations: A Review of 40 Years of Research." *Research in Organizational Behavior* 20: 77–140.

Wolcott, Harry F. 2001. *Writing Up Qualitative Research*. 2d ed. Thousand Oaks, CA: Sage Publications.

Woodward, C. Vann. 1966. *The Strange Career of Jim Crow*. 2d ed. Oxford: Oxford University Press.

Yarbough, Tinsley E. 2002. *Race and Redistricting: The Shaw-Cromartie Cases*. Lawrence: University of Kansas Press.

Young, Iris Marion. 1990. *Justice and the Politics of Difference*. Princeton, NJ: Princeton University Press.

Young, Iris Marion. 2000. *Inclusion and Democracy*. Oxford: Oxford University Press.

Zelizer, Julian E. 2004. *On Capitol Hill: The Struggle to Reform Congress and Its Consequences, 1948–2000*. Cambridge: Cambridge University Press.

Zuberi, Tukufu, and Eduardo Bonilla-Silva, eds. 2008. *White Logic, White Methods: Racism and Methodology*. New York: Rowman and Littlefield.

INDEX